Heidi Martin

Adam Martin

T0357726

DROPPIN' KNOWLEDGE ON SIGHT WORDS AND WORD MAPPING

High-Frequency Word Exercises Aligned to the Science of Reading

JB JOSSEY-BASS™

A Wiley Brand

For general information on our other products and services, please contact our Customer Care Department within the United States at (800) 762-2974, outside the United States at (317) 572-3993. For product technical support, you can find answers to frequently asked questions or reach us via live chat at https://support.wiley.com/s/.

If you believe you've found a mistake in this book, please bring it to our attention by emailing our reader support team at wileysupport@wiley.com with the subject line "Possible Book Errata Submission."

Wiley also publishes its books in a variety of electronic formats. Some content that appears in print may not be available in electronic formats. For more information about Wiley products, visit our website at www.wiley.com.

Library of Congress Control Number: 2025001254 (print)

Cover Design and Images: Wiley

SKY10100169_031425

Contents

Contents

About the Authors

Heidi Martin is trained in LETRS for Early Childhood, IMSE Orton-Gillingham, and Top 10 Tools. She is a National Facilitator for LETRS EC. She has presented at national conferences as well as provided training at the district level. Heidi is the author of *P is for Paint*, which is the one and only alphabet book with embedded mnemonics. She has authored and self-published the *Decodable Adventure* Series books. She taught first grade for over 10 years and most recently taught Kindergarten and 4K.

Adam Martin is a National LETRS Facilitator certified for Units 1–8 and presents to teachers and districts on a weekly basis. He has his Masters in Educational Literacy and his Reading Specialist License. He is the co-author and editor for the *Decodable Adventure* Series books. He taught first grade for seven years and has tutored children of all ages.

How to Contact the Authors

We appreciate your input and questions about this book! Email us at hello@ droppinknowledge.com or visit our website at www.droppinknowledge.com.

Other Books in the *Droppin' Knowledge* Series

Droppin' Knowledge on Phonics: Spelling and Phonics Activities Aligned to the Science of Reading

Droppin' Knowledge on Foundational Skills: Phonological and Phonemic Awareness Activities Aligned to the Science of Reading

Hey, Parents and Teachers!

~~~~~~

We are so excited to help you teach reading! We are Heidi and Adam Martin—both former first-grade teachers (and parents) who now spend our time sharing the Science of Reading with as many people as we can! But before this, we **had no idea there was a science to how we learn to read**. We taught first grade for a combined 15+ years using what most people call "balanced literacy" methods until we found that there is actual science to how we learn to read.

We also learned that according to the 2022 Nation's Report Card, less than 40% of kids are reading proficiently.[1] To us, this was a big wake-up call. If over 60% of our kids are not reading proficiently, we must be doing something wrong!

Once we learned there was decades of evidence and research on how we learn to read, we set out on a mission to unlearn and learn it all. We want to let you know that this has been a journey, not a sprint. There was a lot for us to unlearn (and still is). Throughout this journey of unlearning, we definitely had to work through some ups and downs, as well as emotions of frustration, anger, and regret. The fact that we were not taught this earlier, especially since this science has been around for over 20 years, can really weigh on you. We often think back to the kids we could have helped if we only knew what we know now. However, you don't know better until you do, so we just have to move forward and make sure this doesn't happen again. If some of this is new to you as well, please remember to give yourself grace!

Let's talk about some of the terms we have been using and clarify where we came from and where we are now.

What Is Balanced Literacy?

Balanced literacy sounds good, doesn't it? I mean who doesn't love being balanced? Heidi was sold on this, especially being a type B teacher. She was not a fan of words like "systematic" and "structured." Then, she found out that balanced literacy is not truly balanced after all. Adam was starting his teaching career being taught about the Science of Reading through his licensure program. However, in our school district, we were using balanced literacy curriculums. Going through hours of professional development on this curriculum, this became the norm. Since this was all the buzz, it had to be the most beneficial thing for our

---

[1]https://www.nationsreportcard.gov/reading/nation/achievement/?grade=4.

students, right? Adam said, "I had my skepticisms on balanced literacy, especially since I was seeing minimal progress from my students. I think this is the case for a lot of teachers."

To be clear, when we say balanced literacy, we are talking about programs and strategies that were most often used in schools and called "balanced" within those schools and programs. In reality, these programs skip many of the foundational reading skills kids need in order to become successful readers.

Balanced literacy was supposed to be the answer to the reading wars—a compromise. However, in our experience, there is much more of the whole language approach in balanced literacy programs. We feel that these "balanced literacy" programs are not truly balanced after all. Some examples of the remnants of whole language are

- Skipping a word if you don't know it

- Using meaning or context to solve or read a word

- Believing that reading is natural (aka reading more will help kids become good readers)

- Memorizing "sight words" or spelling words

If our kids cannot decode and read the words on a page (or if they are skipping words), how will they "naturally" become skilled readers? We have learned from the research on how we learn to read that the continuum, or progression of learning to read, is NEVER truly balanced. We spend more time on specific skills when students are developing foundational reading skills than we do later on once those skills and abilities to decode are mastered. The time spent on specific skills will vary based on where our kids are in their reading development. So, although it sounds good, there is never really a "balance" to literacy.

What Is the Science of Reading?

You have probably heard the term "Science of Reading" more times than you can count, but the definition can get a little muddy. So let's talk about what the Science of Reading is **not**.

The Science of Reading is not a curriculum.

The Science of Reading is not just phonics.

The Science of Reading is not a strategy or activity.

Here is how The Reading League defines the Science of Reading[2]:

The Science of Reading is a vast, interdisciplinary body of scientifically based research about reading and issues related to reading and writing. This research has been conducted over the last five decades across the world.

It is derived from thousands of studies conducted in multiple languages. The Science of Reading has culminated in a preponderance of evidence to inform how proficient reading and writing develop, why some have difficulty, and how we can most effectively assess and teach and, therefore, improve student outcomes through prevention of and intervention for reading difficulties.

The Science of Reading is derived from researchers from multiple fields:

Cognitive psychology

Communication sciences

Developmental psychology

Education

Implementation science

Linguistics

Neuroscience

School psychology

To break that down, we like to say that **the Science of Reading is the research and the evidence on how our brains learn to read**. This means that not just one study is referenced when discussing the skills kids need to read. Again, this is research that has been conducted for almost 50 years and includes research of the research (meta-analysis)!

---

[2]https://www.thereadingleague.org/wp-content/uploads/2022/03/Science-of-Reading-eBook-2022.pdf.

We hope that helps explain some of the terms you may have been hearing about and why we decided to write these books. We are so excited for you to use these activities with your students and/or your own children. We have done the research and can assure you that the methods used in this book are more effective than memorization.

We created these activities to help you teach words in a brain-friendly way! You will find activities for tricky high-frequency words, cheat sheets for teaching over 230 high-frequency words, word mapping pages for spelling words, and mapping mats that make word mapping fun!

Both of us were first-grade teachers and most of our teaching revolved around getting kids to learn a set of 100 words. (While we only worked on 100 words throughout the year, we have heard that some schools require much more!) This was something that we spent the majority of the year teaching. We would introduce several words, play games, spell the words, put them on the word wall, and review them daily.

Some of our favorite games to play were silly sticks, BANG!, musical sight word chairs, and bingo. Silly sticks were simply popsicle sticks that we wrote a fun movement on. We would have a student randomly choose a stick and we would do the action to spell our new word. We love anything that gets kids up and moving so this was a favorite!

BANG! was a game that kids played in a center. They would choose a card, read a word, and if they knew it, they would keep it. If they got BANG!, they would have to put all their cards back.

Musical sight word chairs is just like musical chairs, but once the music stops and the kid finds a chair, there would be a book with specific sight words the students had to read and find in that book.

Bingo is self-explanatory, but it was definitely another favorite!

All of these games were fun and engaging for kids, **but kids would still leave us at the end of the year not knowing all 100 sight words!** How could this be after we had spent so much time on them and had so much fun with them? Even the students that did show progress in learning most of the words went to the next grade and would not remember them. This frustrated us, frustrated the kids, frustrated the teachers in the next grade, and I am sure it was frustrating for their parents as well.

As we started to learn more about the evidence we have on how we learn to read and how our brains work when we read, we learned that **memorizing words can take hundreds of repetitions.** Depending on the child, memorizing a word can take around 5–500 repetitions. Thinking back, while it felt like we must have reviewed each word 500 times, did we really? It is likely that the kids who left us still not knowing all 100 words are the kids who needed more repetitions. Not to mention the fact that we were not giving them the skills they need to decode new, unknown words!

If any of this sounds familiar, you are in the right place! This book was written to give you some background into how we learn words and the tools to teach them.

Let's talk about the term SIGHT WORD. *For many years, we told parents and students that a sight word is a word that just has to be memorized.* You have to know it by sight because it is not spelled how we might expect it to be. That is why we believed it was called a sight word. We found out later that we were wrong.

Let us share the definitions we have learned along our Science of Reading journey.

What Is a Sight Word?

The definition that researchers use is that **a sight word is ANY word you can read effortlessly and automatically without sounding it out or guessing**. This is because your brain has already made the neuron connections of the sound–symbol relationship of that word, called orthographic mapping, and has stored that word in your brain. Adults actually know 30,000–70,000 sight words. All the words you are reading in this book right now are sight words for you, because you know them effortlessly and automatically. As soon as you see the word, you know it. You are not trying to use a picture to help you solve a word. You are not sounding out every single word. These are words that are stored in what's called your orthographic lexicon.

So while the words in the activity pages may not actually be sight words for your kids yet, our goal is to turn them into sight words! We want our kids to know these words effortlessly and automatically so that they can read them with ease. This ease and fluency then frees up space in our kids' brains to begin to understand what they are reading, instead of spending all their brain energy on trying to figure out what the words are. The activities in this book will help you do just that!

What Is a High-Frequency Word?

Okay so we admit it, we definitely used to use the terms *sight word* and *high-frequency word* interchangeably, but they are not necessarily the same. High-frequency words are the words that we see most often in text. These are the words we were trying to get our students to memorize. These are the words that are on our word walls. These are the words that kids need to know in order to read most texts. These are the words in the activities included in this book!

Again, when we teach high-frequency words, the goal is to turn these words into sight words. In our experience, unlearning this, especially if you are a teacher like us who did this for so many years, can be very overwhelming. Just remember that change takes time. Our hope is that the activities in this book will help you take steps toward that change.

Let's do a little activity to illustrate the difference between sight words and high-frequency words. The following list of words are likely words that you'll be able to read right away. Try to read this set of words and pay attention to whether or not you were able to read these words effortlessly and automatically.

plant	house	video
grateful	grass	refrigerator
dog	animate	curtain
television	heater	

If you could read this list of words effortlessly and automatically without sounding them out or guessing, these are sight words for you. However, **these are not high-frequency words.** These are not words a kindergartener or a first grader will have on their word wall or "sight word" list.

That is the difference between high-frequency words and sight words.

This can sometimes be a tricky concept so let's try it this way. Set a timer for one minute and on the next few lines, write down as many words as you can think of that are sight words for you but not high-frequency words.

_____

_____

_____

_____

This may or may not have been difficult for you, but it is definitely something we overlook and do not think of as competent readers, educators, or parents. Now let's try another set of words. I want you to try to read these words and see if you can read them just as fast as you were able to read the previous list.

dehydroascorbic

tocopherol

cobalamin

acetylsalicylic

hippopotomonstrosesquippedaliophobia

Okay so that last one is just for fun because it means "fear of long words"!

Unless you are in the field of nutrition or medicine, these words were likely trickier for you and took you a bit longer. You could likely sound them out because you have decoding skills; however, you could not read them effortlessly and automatically without sounding them out or guessing. That means these words are not sight words for you.

Now I will show you one more list you have likely seen before. These are the lists that many of us had our kids memorize. This list of words[3] we typically call "sight words" is actually a list of high-frequency words. (That means none of these words should be on your list you created above!)

Pre-primer: (40 words) a, and, away, big, blue, can, come, down, find, for, funny, go, help, here, I, in, is, it, jump, little, look, make, me, my, not, one, play, red, run, said, see, the, three, to, two, up, we, where, yellow, you

Primer: (52 words) all, am, are, at, ate, be, black, brown, but, came, did, do, eat, four, get, good, have, he, into, like, must, new, no, now, on, our, out, please,

---

[3]These are taken from the Dolch sight words list, developed by educator Dr. Edward Dolch beginning in 1936 and eventually published in his book _Problems in Reading_ (1948, Garrard Press).

pretty, ran, ride, saw, say, she, so, soon, that, there, they, this, too, under, want, was, well, went, what, white, who, will, with, yes

1st Grade: (41 words) after, again, an, any, as, ask, by, could, every, fly, from, give, going, had, has, her, him, his, how, just, know, let, live, may, of, old, once, open, over, put, round, some, stop, take, thank, them, then, think, walk, were, when

2nd Grade: (46 words) always, around, because, been, before, best, both, buy, call, cold, does, don't, fast, first, five, found, gave, goes, green, its, made, many, off, or, pull, read, right, sing, sit, sleep, tell, their, these, those, upon, us, use, very, wash, which, why, wish, work, would, write, your

3rd Grade: (41 words) about, better, bring, carry, clean, cut, done, draw, drink, eight, fall, far, full, got, grow, hold, hot, hurt, if, keep, kind, laugh, light, long, much, myself, never, only, own, pick, seven, shall, show, six, small, start, ten, today, together, try, warm

We want to turn these high-frequency words into sight words, **but they are not considered sight words until we can read them effortlessly and automatically without sounding them out or guessing.**

Many of us in the teacher world like to say, "Every word wants to be a sight word when it grows up!"

What Are Heart Words?

Heart word is a newer term that has become popular over the past few years. A heart word refers to a word with an irregular sound–spelling pattern. For example, the word "said" is referred to as a heart word because the -AI is not a normal spelling for the short E /ĕ/ sound.

It is very important to note that only 4% of words are truly irregular. Most words are actually not heart words at all. They become heart words when we try to teach them before we teach the phonics pattern. We want to avoid this whenever possible by teaching skills before words.

How Do We Do That?

The easiest way to start is to organize your high-frequency words by phonics skill. I have done this and let me tell you, I was shocked to see how many words from my word wall could fit perfectly into a phonics scope and sequence. Why was I teaching the word GET as a tricky word kids had to memorize instead of just teaching it when I taught short E words?

I have included my high-frequency word scope and sequence in this book for you. *Please note that it is meant to be a working document and you should adjust it as needed.*

Once we have our words sorted, how will we get our kids to learn these words? The answer is something called orthographic mapping. I'll be honest ... I wanted nothing to do with this term when I first heard it. This is one of those researcher terms so let me break it down for you.

What in the World Is Orthographic Mapping?

Orthographic mapping is the process that happens in our brains when we teach kids words in a way that aligns with how our brains read. Orthographic mapping is not something that we do, and it is not something that we have our kids do. It is a cognitive process of permanently storing words by going through the process of connecting sounds to letters/letter patterns.

Oftentimes when people hear this, they say, "yeah that's great but there are still words that have to be memorized." This is not necessarily true so we think it is helpful to share some of the studies that really helped drive this point home. For us, it really helped us to learn that our brains just do not read whole words.

The first thing we want to share is this excerpt from cognitive neuroscientist Stanislas Dehaene. In his book *Reading in the Brain*, he says that whole word reading is a myth. He says that as adults, we have the illusion that we are reading whole words because our brains get lightning fast at matching sounds to symbols. But he emphasizes that this is an illusion, and we are still reading by matching those sounds to symbols. He also discusses how this looks different in kindergarten and first grade. Kids are much slower at this, so if you are a teacher or a parent of a kindergartener or a first-grade student who is laboriously blending words sound by sound, just know that is part of the development of learning how to read.

> "There is no longer any reason to doubt that the global contours of words play virtually no role in reading. We do not recognize a printed word through a holistic grasping of its contour, but because our brain breaks it down into letters and graphemes. The letterbox area in our left occipito temporal cortex processes all of a word's letters in parallel.[4]"

---

[4]Dehaene, S. 2009. *Reading in the Brain: The New Science of How We Read*. p. 224. (New York: Penguin Random House).

Another study[5] we want to share with you is from Bruce McCandless. Bruce conducted an experiment where he invented a fake alphabet and taught this alphabet in different ways to two different groups of people. With one group, he taught them by having them memorize whole words. This is similar to what happens with our kids when we teach them whole words before they know the letters. Bruce did not explain what the symbols meant. He just put them together in strings of symbols and had the participants memorize those whole words. With the other group, Bruce took the time to teach them the features of each symbol. So what happened? Well, at first, the group that only memorized the whole words did better than the second group. On day two, the first group started to forget the first set of words when they were asked to memorize another set of words. This cycle continued to happen. The first group forgot more and more words as they memorized new words. Meanwhile, the second group, who learned what the symbols meant, made steady progress and could soon read far more words than the first group. This is because they could decode the words as they had learned the sounds and symbols, which opened the door for them to read more words.

The last thing we want to share with you is the research from Dr. Linnea Ehri on orthographic mapping.

> "Orthographic mapping (OM) involves the formation of letter-sound connections to bond the spellings, pronunciations, and meanings of specific words in memory. It explains how children learn to read words by sight, to spell words from memory, and to acquire vocabulary words from print. This development is portrayed by Ehri . . . as a sequence of overlapping phases, each characterized by the predominant type of connection linking spellings of words to their pronunciations in memory. During development, the connections improve in quality and word-learning value, from visual nonalphabetic, to partial alphabetic, to full grapho-phonemic, to consolidated grapho-syllabic and grapho-morphemic. OM is enabled by phonemic awareness and grapheme-phoneme knowledge. Recent findings indicate that OM to support sight word reading is facilitated when beginners are taught about articulatory features of phonemes and when grapheme-phoneme relations are taught with letter-embedded picture mnemonics.

---

[5]https://news.stanford.edu/stories/2015/05/stanford-study-on-brain-waves-shows-how-different-teaching-methods-affect-reading-development.

Vocabulary learning is facilitated when spellings accompany pronunciations and meanings of new words to activate OM. Teaching students the strategy of pronouncing novel words aloud as they read text silently activates OM and helps them build their vocabularies. Because spelling-sound connections are retained in memory, they impact the processing of phonological constituents and phonological memory for words.[6]"

To connect to what Dr. Ehri stated above, the more our students know and learn about a word, the richer, or deeper, that word is stored in their reading brain. Discussing syllables and sounds of the word, spelling patterns of that word, meaning (or meanings) of that word, and how that word is used in context all give students a deeper understanding of that word. This will be beneficial as students encounter new words, because of the orthographic mapping that has occurred, they will use those known spelling patterns to decode and spell new words.

One of the most effective ways that we have found to teach kids words is by having them match sounds to symbols. That means breaking apart the sounds in a word, listening for each sound, and then spelling that sound. The science of our reading brain shows us that we must know the sounds to connect the letter or spelling pattern to that sound. We are genetically and naturally meant to learn and acquire sounds/speech and then can connect to print. **Stick with us because this still works for tricky words like "said" and "the."**

The technical term is phoneme–grapheme mapping. A phoneme is a sound, and a grapheme is a letter or group of letters representing a sound. For example, break apart the sounds you hear in the word "play." The sounds are /p/ /l/ /ā/, so those are the phonemes. Now to spell each of those sounds, we need some graphemes. The grapheme that spells /p/ is the letter -P. The grapheme that spells /l/ is the letter -L, and the grapheme that spells the long -A or /ā/ is the letters -AY. As you can see, the wordplay, while it has four letters, it only has three graphemes.

---

[6]Ehri, L.C. 2014. "Orthographic Mapping in the Acquisition of Sight Word Reading, Spelling Memory, and Vocabulary Learning." *Scientific Studies of Reading* 18 (1): 5–21, doi: https://doi.org/10.1080/10888438.2013.819356.

Word	Letters	Phonemes	Graphemes
play	p,l,a,y	/p/ /l/ /ā/	p - l - ay
chip	c,h,i,p	/ch/ /ĭ/ /p/	ch - i - p
cow	c,o,w	/k/ /ow/	c - ow
said	s,a,i,d	/s/ /ĕ/ /d/	s - ai - d
laugh	l,a,u,g,h	/l/ /ă/ /f/	l - au - gh
city	c,i,t,y	/s/ /ĭ/ /t/ /ē/	c - i - t - y
duck	d,u,c,k	/d/ /ŭ/ /k/	d - u - ck

When you see a straight line over a sound, it means the vowel is long (aka it says its letter name). When you see a curved line over a sound, it means the vowel sound is short.

Here is the process that we follow for teaching kids all words. This includes high-frequency words and spelling words.

Step 1: Say the word and have the child repeat the word.

We personally do not like to show the word before we map it because we do not want our students to simply copy the word and skip this whole process. Again, our reading brains work speech to print, so we discuss sounds first. Otherwise, we have wasted our time. Some sources will have you show the word first, but again, we like to have the child say the word without actually seeing the word.

Have students say the word.

said

Step 2: Have the child break apart the sounds.

Step 2 is all about listening to each sound in the word. A child needs to be able to break apart these sounds before they are ready to learn words. If a child struggles to do this, you may need to stop and return to phonemic awareness.

Then have them break apart the sounds.

/s/ /e/ /d/

Step 3: Have the child spell each sound.

Another essential skill for kids to be ready to learn words is to know how sounds are spelled. A child may struggle with this process without phonemic awareness and letter sound skills.

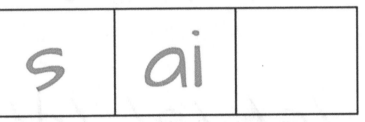

Then have them spell each sound.

s	ai	

Step 4: Teach any irregular sound–spelling patterns.

Step 4 really shows the difference between memorizing and mapping words. When we have kids just memorize words, we do not talk about any of the features of the word. We may have spelled the word, but we did not talk about the sounds or point out how the sounds are spelled. The problem with skipping this is that our brains read by matching sounds to symbols. If we cut all that out, we do our kids a disservice.

Teach any irregular sound spellings.

lay - laid
pay - paid
say - said

old english used 'saith' & it is possible that
long ago said was pronounced as say - d!

In this step, we want to talk about the irregular sound spelling. If we can explain it, we should do that. Many times if a word has an irregular spelling pattern, it is usually due to it being an older word that was influenced, or came from, a different language. English has a lot of influences from different languages, especially Anglo-Saxon, French, Latin, and Greek. We have changed the way we say those words, for ease of speech, but the spelling remains the same.

You may see many people use a heart to help kids remember this part. Just be mindful of what we already discussed about heart words. I will often have kids circle the spelling or underline it … whatever works to help them notice that irregular part.

Step 5: Segment and Blend the Sounds

Finally, you will have kids repeat the sounds and then blend those sounds together to read the word they just spelled. This reinforces the sounds in the words and practices blending those sounds, which, again, is how our brains read. See the following link: https://droppinknowledge.com/topics/sight-words/.

This is the process we will follow in the activity pages for high-frequency words with irregular parts. Our goal is to turn all of these words into sight words using these activities. With this process, it typically takes just a couple of repetitions before the word is permanently stored; however, some kids will require more practice. Plus by following this process, you are continuing practicing the basic decoding skills of sounds to letters/letter patterns, which will in turn give kids the foundation to be able to apply those skills to decode and spell new/unknown words.

Pro-tip: If a child is having difficulty remembering a word after mapping it several times, be sure to check that they have the necessary foundational skills.

"To form connections and retain words in memory, readers need some requisite abilities. They must possess phonemic awareness (i.e., the ability to focus on and manipulate phonemes in speech), particularly segmentation and blending. They must know the major grapheme-phoneme correspondences of the writing system. Application of these strategies activates orthographic mappings to retain the words' spellings, pronunciations, and meanings in memory. [David] Share . . . referred to this as a self-teaching mechanism. With repeated readings that activate orthographic mapping, written words are retained in memory to support reading and spelling."
—Linnea Ehri[7]

Kids must have phonemic awareness and knowledge of letters and sounds. If you find your children or students are struggling with this, check out our book *Droppin' Knowledge on Foundational Skills* for activities to help solidify these skills.

To get started teaching high-frequency words, it is helpful to sort the words by phonics skills. This way we are following the sounds and phonics skills students have learned. The following scope and sequence contains 236 high-frequency words sorted by phonics skills. As you may notice, many of the words here are perfectly regular and decodable! The regularly spelled words can be taught using the sound box template and/or mapping mats (found in the back of this book).

We created this scope and sequence by comparing various phonics programs that are aligned with research and our experience teaching first grade.

---

[7]Ehri, L.C. 2014. "Orthographic Mapping in the Acquisition of Sight Word Reading, Spelling Memory, and Vocabulary Learning." *Scientific Studies of Reading* 18 (1): 5–21, doi: https://doi.org/10.1080/ 10888438.2013.819356.

If you absolutely need to teach a word before it comes up in the scope and sequence, you can make it a temporary heart word. Be sure students understand that it is not an irregular spelling, they just have not learned it yet. We really try to keep this to a minimum!

The words included in this list are 220 Dolch Words, 100 Fry Words, CKLA Word lists, and F&P words. All words are sorted by sound. Some words like "those" come later in the sequence because if we put it in with TH words, kids will have trouble with it because they have not yet learned the other phonics skills in the word. By the time you get to the word "those," students will have learned the TH digraph and that /z/ can be spelled with an S. Now they have the skills they need to read the whole word.

We tried to have as few heart words as possible!

> **PLEASE NOTE:** We tried to place heart words closest to their phonetic patterns as we could but please know not all of them fit nicely. For example, "said" and "been" both have the short E sound, so we put them with those words. "To" and "do" sound like the vowel team /oo/; however, those words are needed well before you would teach that sound–spelling pattern. Therefore, we sprinkled them where we thought they would fit best.

If you feel that a word makes more sense in a different place, please feel free to adjust as needed for your students or children.

High-Frequency Words Sorted by Sound

SKILL	High-Frequency Words	Heart Words
Short A	at, and, an, can, am, had, ask, ran, fast	the
Short E	get, red, yes, ten, went, let, help, best	said, been
Short I	it, in, if, its, big, did, sit, him, six	to, into
Short O	on, not, hot, got, off, stop, mom	want, do
Short U	up, us, cut, run, but, jump, just, must, upon	of, from
Long Vowel	a**, be, he, me, no, so, we, I, go, open	little, you
Digraph (th)	with, this, that, than, then, them, both	two
Digraph (sh)	she, wish	should, could, would
Digraph (wh)	when	who, wash, what
Digraph (ch)	which, much	laugh
Digraph (ng)	long, going, sing, bring	some, come
Floss Rule	well, tell, will, shall	put
Ending Blend (nk)	drink, thank, think	again
Ending Digraph (ck)	black, pick	done
S as /z/	as, has, is, his	does, goes, was
VCe	use, ate, came, made, make, take, gave, five, like, ride, time, white, here, those, these, live**, have*, give*	write, one, once
Vowel Team (ee)	see, green, keep, sleep, three	seven
Vowel Team (ea)	eat, read**, clean, each, please	
Vowel Team (ay)	say, play, way, day, may, away	they, today
Vowel Team (ow)	grow, show, own, yellow	know, don't
Vowel Team (igh)	right, light	eight
L- Controlled	all, fall, ball, small, full, pull, also, always	walk
Closed Syllable Exceptions	kind, old, cold, hold, find	
Bossy R (ar)	far, part, start	are, carry, warm
Bossy R (or)	or, for, more, before	work, your, four
Bossy R (er) *most common	her, hers, after, under, better, number, over, never	very, were, together, other, every
Bossy R (ir) (ur)	first, hurt, girl	there, where, their
Tricky Y (as E)	funny, only	many, any, pretty
Tricky Y (as I)	my, why, by, fly, try, sky, myself	buy
Vowel Digraph (oo)	too, soon	new, blue
Vowel Digraph (oo)	good, look, took	
Vowel Digraph (aw)	saw, draw	because
Diphthong (ow)	how, now, down, brown	
Diphthong (ou)	round, about, out, our, found	

*Another job of silent E is to make sure no word ends in a V.
**Can be pronounced 2 ways.

@droppinknowledgewithheidi

We have also included cheat sheets for you on how to map every word included in this scope and sequence. You can find them in the back of the book.

The "Mapping Mats" pages contain activity sheets that you can use to teach each high-frequency word with "tricky" spellings. You should still follow the same process of having kids say the word, count and say the sounds, and then spell the sounds.

We recommend mapping the word together first using the sound boxes or mapping mats. We created mapping mats as a fun twist on sound boxes. Word mapping centers can work all year and regular sound boxes can get boring! You can also use these to "spice up" your small group time! They work the same as sound boxes. Use manipulatives to have students segment and count each sound in a word. Place the manipulatives on the images. Then, have students use the boxes to spell each sound. Finally, have them blend and write the word on the lines. You can have students color their mapping mats and laminate them for multiple uses. We like to use the same mats for about a month or so and then switch them up.

> **Please note if you are working with words with more than four sounds, you can use the sound box template. You can also find more mapping mats with three, four, and five sound boxes on Heidi's website at www.droppinknowledge.com and within the LitFlix Club.**

Once you have done this with the students, you can use the following pages as more practice.

Please note that the boxes will not always be the correct number. Kids should segment each sound verbally and/or with tapping and then have them decide how many boxes they will be using. To help students with this, and bring in a multi-sensory approach to learning, you can use manipulatives such as counting chips (and you can be creative depending on the season and/or your students' interests. For example, instead of chips, you could use toy cars, gems, cotton balls, etc.)! This multimodal approach will help reinforce the sounds of the word and also allow them to see how many sounds or boxes are needed when segmenting that word.

Count the Sounds

Spell the Sounds

Write the Word

Count the Sounds

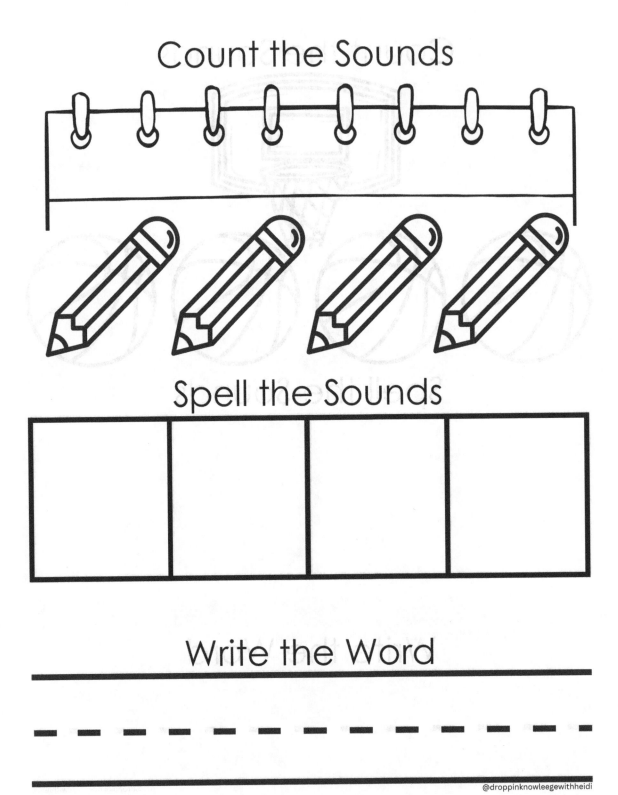

Spell the Sounds

Write the Word

Count the Sounds

Spell the Sounds

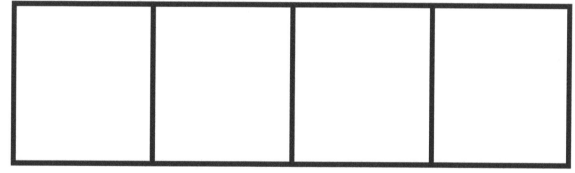

Write the Word

_____

- - - - - - - - - - -

_____

Count the Sounds

Spell the Sounds

Write the Word

@droppinknowleegewithheidi

Count the Sounds

Spell the Sounds

Write the Word

- - - - - - - - - - - - - - -

Count the Sounds

Spell the Sounds

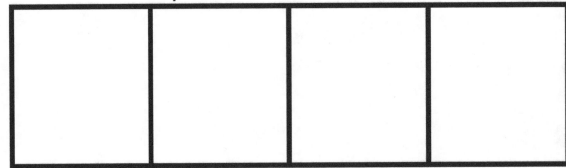

Write the Word

@droppinknowleegewithheidi

Count the Sounds

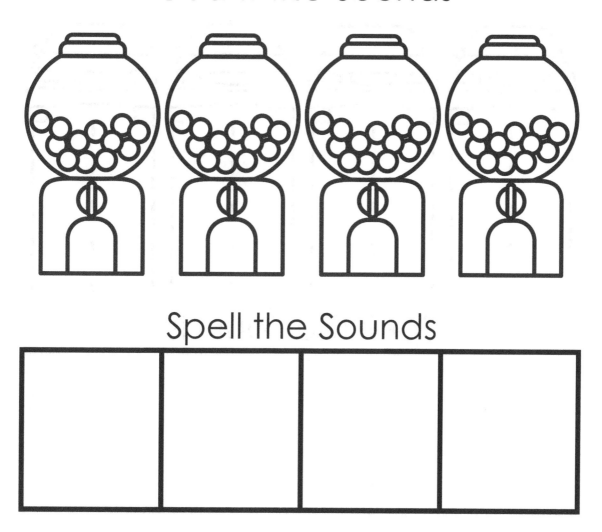

Spell the Sounds

Write the Word

Count the Sounds

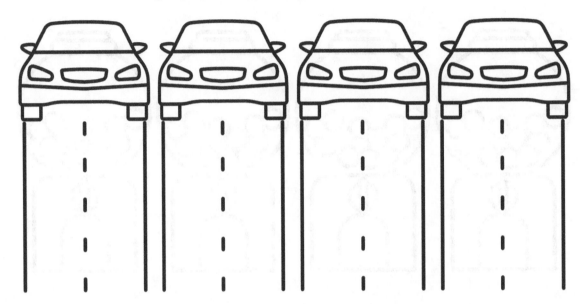

Spell the Sounds

Write the Word

@droppinknowleegewithheidi

Count the Sounds

Spell the Sounds

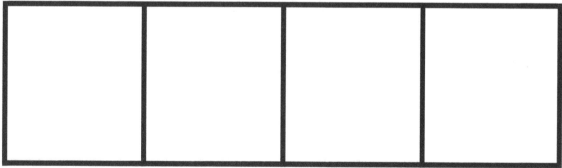

Write the Word

Count the Sounds

Spell the Sounds

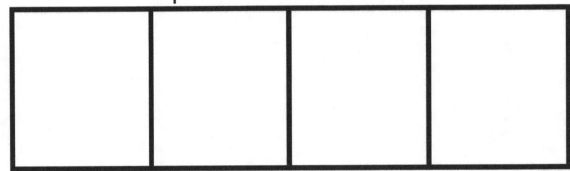

Write the Word

Count the Sounds

Spell the Sounds

Write the Word

Count the Sounds

Spell the Sounds

Write the Word

@droppinknowleegewithheidi

Count the Sounds

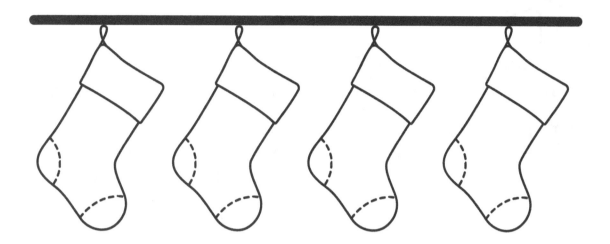

Spell the Sounds

Write the Word

Count the Sounds

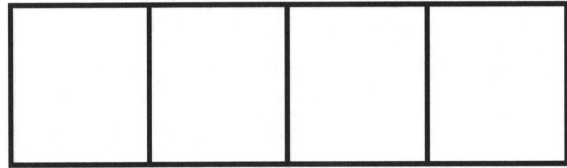

Spell the Sounds

Write the Word

Count the Sounds

Spell the Sounds

Write the Word

Count the Sounds

Spell the Sounds

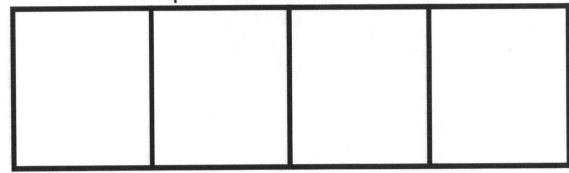

Write the Word

Count the Sounds

Spell the Sounds

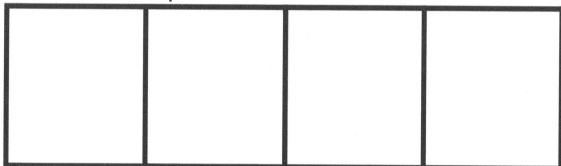

Write the Word

Count the Sounds

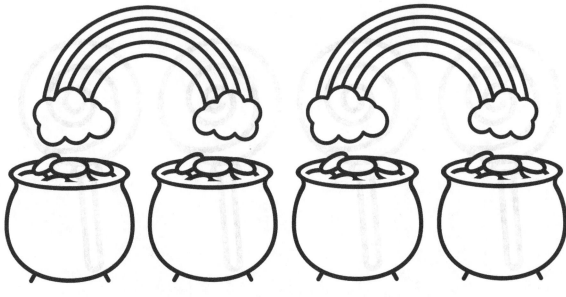

Spell the Sounds

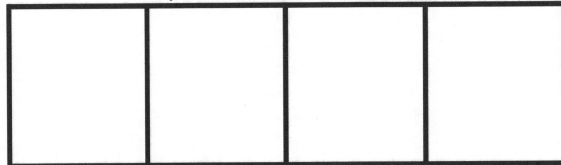

Write the Word

Count the Sounds

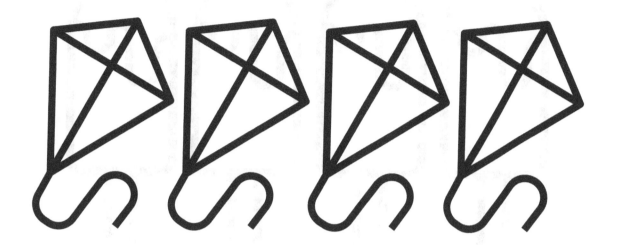

Spell the Sounds

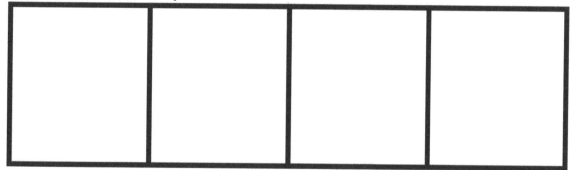

Write the Word

_____

- - - - - - - - - - - - - - - -

_____

Count the Sounds

Spell the Sounds

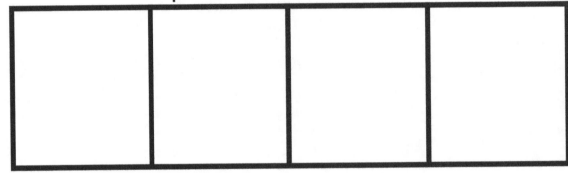

Write the Word

Count the Sounds

Spell the Sounds

Write the Word

Count the Sounds

Spell the Sounds

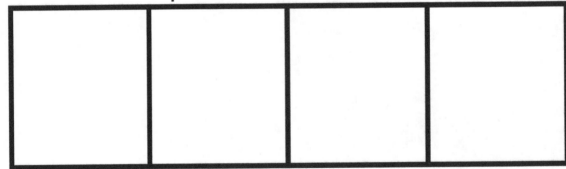

Write the Word

Count the Sounds

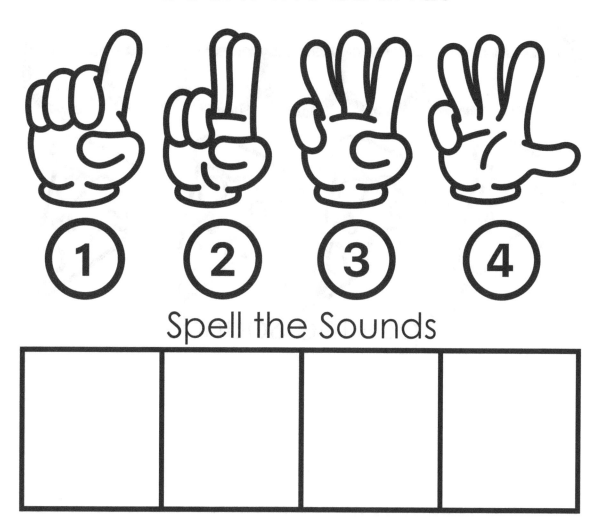

Spell the Sounds

Write the Word

Count the Sounds

Spell the Sounds

Write the Word

Count the Sounds

Spell the Sounds

Write the Word

_ _ _ _ _ _ _ _ _ _ _ _ _ _ _ _ _ _ _

Mapping words is not just for high-frequency words. We can have students map their spelling words as well!

> During my first year of teaching, I gave weekly spelling tests. Thinking back on those tests, I realized that the words I tested my kids on were completely random. I remember testing my kids on all the Vowel-R (or bossy R) words at once. At that time, I had not explicitly taught those phonics skills to my students. (I actually was not explicitly teaching phonics at all!) —Heidi

Adam's experience was very similar. Taking words that were told by the curriculum to have the students practice throughout the week, and then test them on Friday. Those words did not revolve around a specific skill and/or were too advanced for the majority of his students, due to the fact that there was no specific phonics instruction incorporated within the curriculum. Phonics was a supplement and an afterthought.

The problem with this is that when we give kids a list of spelling words to practice for the week, test them on Friday, and then move on, we essentially ask them to memorize those words for a short period. Since this is not aligned with how our brains learn to read, kids will forget these words the following week. It can also be problematic to test kids on words that have phonics patterns that have not been explicitly taught yet. Again, when we do this, we ask kids to memorize words and spelling patterns. We know memorization can take hundreds of repetitions. It is not something that is going to be mastered in just one week.

So what do we do instead?

We should align our spelling words with the phonics skills we teach. Our high-frequency words can fit right into these lists as well!

For example, if I am teaching short E during our phonics lessons, then my spelling words for that week should be words with that spelling pattern. I can include high-frequency words like get or red in this list because they follow that phonics pattern. It is important here to follow a scope and sequence so you're not accidentally testing kids on words with phonics patterns you haven't taught yet.

We should also have kids practice their spelling words through phoneme–grapheme mapping.

This is a reminder that a phoneme is a sound, and a grapheme is the letter or letters that spell each sound. So when kids are working on their words for the week, we don't want to give them practice activities where they're focusing on the shape of the word or the look of the word in any way. We want them to practice these words in a way that aligns with how our brains read, and that is by matching sounds to symbols or phonemes to graphemes.

By making these changes to how you practice and assess spelling, you will see that your kids are much more successful in both reading and writing these words. For more information and resources on these skills, check out our book *Droppin' Knowledge on Phonics & Spelling*.

On the following pages, you will see word mapping pages for most of the phonics skills in the scope and sequence. *(If you do not see a page for a skill, it is because there are not enough decodable words with that phonics pattern yet. Remember, we do not want to include words like THRONE for TH because according to the scope and sequence, kids have not yet learned about the silent E.)* These pages will give kids the practice they need with each specific skill. It will also help with their spelling of words with this phonics pattern as they will be practicing in a brain-friendly way!

Say it, Map it, Write it, and Read it!

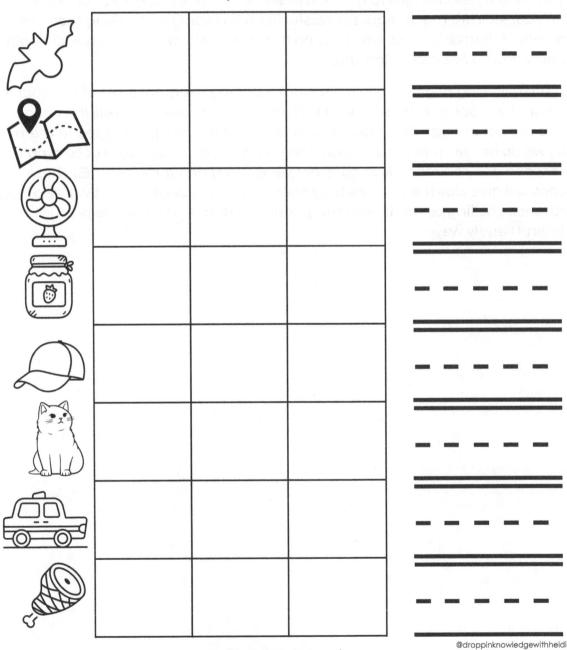

Short A Words

@droppinknowledgewithheidi

ANSWER KEY

b	a	t
m	a	p
f	a	n
j	a	m
h	a	t
c	a	t
c	a	b
h	a	m

Short A Words

Say it, Map it,
Write it, and Read it!

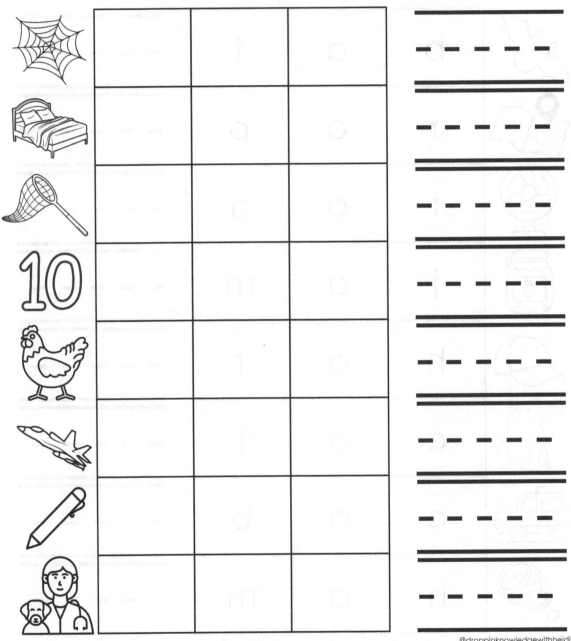

Short E Words

@droppinknowledgewithheidi

ANSWER KEY

w	e	b
b	e	d
n	e	t
t	e	n
h	e	n
j	e	t
p	e	n
v	e	t

Short E Words

@droppinknowledgewithheidi

Say it, Map it, Write it, and Read it!

Short I Words

ANSWER KEY

p	i	n
p	i	g
f	i	n
b	i	b
r	i	b
d	i	g
k	i	t
l	i	p

Short I Words

Say it, Map it, Write it, and Read it!

Short O Words

@droppinknowledgewithheidi

ANSWER KEY

t	o	p
l	o	g
h	o	t
m	o	p
c	o	p
p	o	t
r	o	d
p	o	d

Short O Words

@droppinknowledgewithheidi

Say it, Map it, Write it, and Read it!

Short U Words

ANSWER KEY

s	u	n
n	u	t
c	u	t
m	u	g
b	u	s
b	u	n
r	u	n
h	u	t

Short U Words

@droppinknowledgewithheidi

Say it, Map it, Write it, and Read it!

Write a sentence using one of the words above.

Digraph TH Words

ANSWER KEY

m	a	th	
s	l	o	th
b	a	th	
m	o	th	
p	a	th	

Write a sentence using one of the words above.

Digraph TH Words

Say it, Map it, Write it, and Read it!

Digraph CH Words

ANSWER KEY

l	u	n	ch	
b	r	a	n	ch
ch	i	n		
ch	o	p		
ch	a	t		
ch	i	p	s	
b	e	n	ch	
p	i	n	ch	

Digraph CH Words

Say it, Map it, Write it, and Read it!

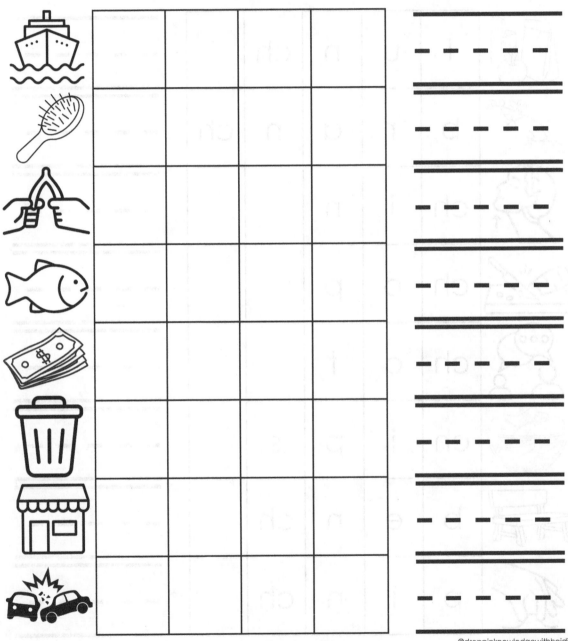

Digraph SH Words

ANSWER KEY

sh	i	p	
b	r	u	sh
w	i	sh	
f	i	sh	
c	a	sh	
t	r	a	sh
sh	o	p	
c	r	a	sh

Digraph SH Words

@droppinknowledgewithheidi

Say it, Map it, Write it, and Read it!

Floss Words

ANSWER KEY

b	u	ll	
s	m	e	ll
b	e	ll	
sh	e	ll	
b	u	zz	
y	e	ll	
c	l	i	ff
p	r	e	ss

Floss Words

@droppinknowledgewithheidi

Say it, Map it,
Write it, and Read it!

NK & NG Words

ANSWER KEY

b	a	n	k
t	a	n	k
d	u	n	k
w	i	ng	
s	o	ng	
s	i	n	k
w	i	n	k
s	i	ng	

NK & NG Words

@droppinknowledgewithheidi

Say it, Map it, Write it, and Read it!

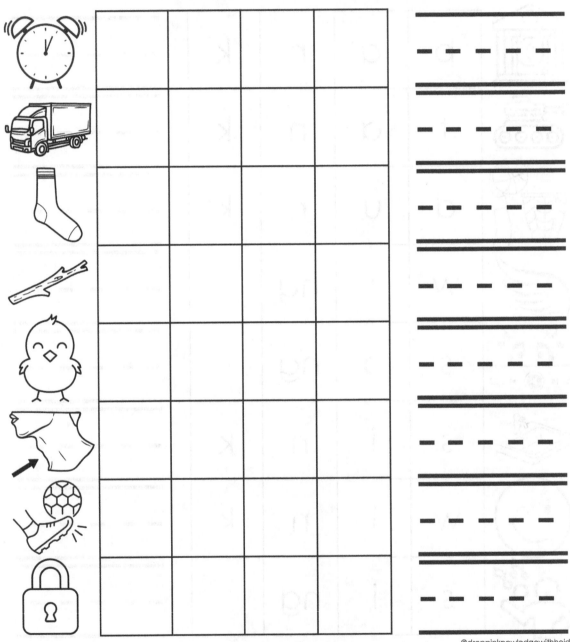

Digraph CK Words

@droppinknowledgewithheidi

ANSWER KEY

c	l	o	ck
t	r	u	ck
s	o	ck	
s	t	i	ck
ch	i	ck	
n	e	ck	
k	i	ck	
l	o	ck	

Digraph CK Words

@droppinknowledgewithheidi

Say it, Map it, Write it, and Read it!

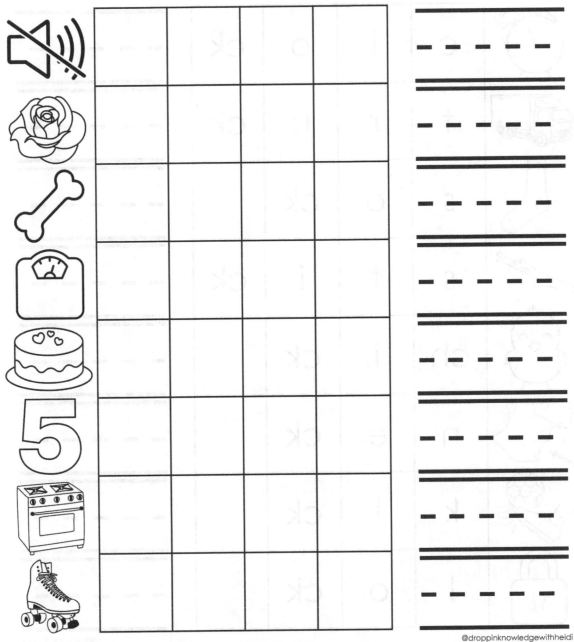

Silent E Words

@droppinknowledgewithheidi

ANSWER KEY

m	u	te	
r	o	se	
b	o	ne	
s	c	a	le
c	a	ke	
f	i	ve	
s	t	o	ve
s	k	a	te

Silent E Words

@droppinknowledgewithheidi

Say it, Map it,
Write it, and Read it!

Vowel Team EE

ANSWER KEY

f	ee	t	
b	ee		
h	ee	l	
q	u	ee	n
s	ee	d	s
b	ee	t	
ch	ee	se	
t	ee	th	

Vowel Team EE

@droppinknowledgewithheidi

Say it, Map it, Write it, and Read it!

Vowel Team EA

ANSWER KEY

b	ea	n	
r	ea	d	
b	ea	ch	
l	ea	f	
t	ea		
b	ea	d	s
t	r	ea	t
ea	t		

Vowel Team EA

Say it, Map it, Write it, and Read it!

Vowel Teams AY & AI

ANSWER KEY

p	ay		
h	ay		
r	ai	n	
t	r	ay	
p	ai	n	t
ch	ai	n	
p	l	ay	
t	r	ai	n

Vowel Teams AY & AI

Say it, Map it, Write it, and Read it!

Vowel Team OW

ANSWER KEY

p	i	ll	ow	
e	l	b	ow	
r	ai	n	b	ow
th	r	ow		
t	ow			
s	n	ow		
c	r	ow		
r	ow			

Vowel Team OW

@droppinknowledgewithheidi

Say it, Map it, Write it, and Read it!

Write a sentence using one of the words above.

_____

_____

_____

Vowel Team IGH

ANSWER KEY

n	igh	t
r	igh	t
l	igh	t
f	igh	t
th	igh	

Write a sentence using one of the words above.

Vowel Team IGH

Say it, Map it, Write it, and Read it!

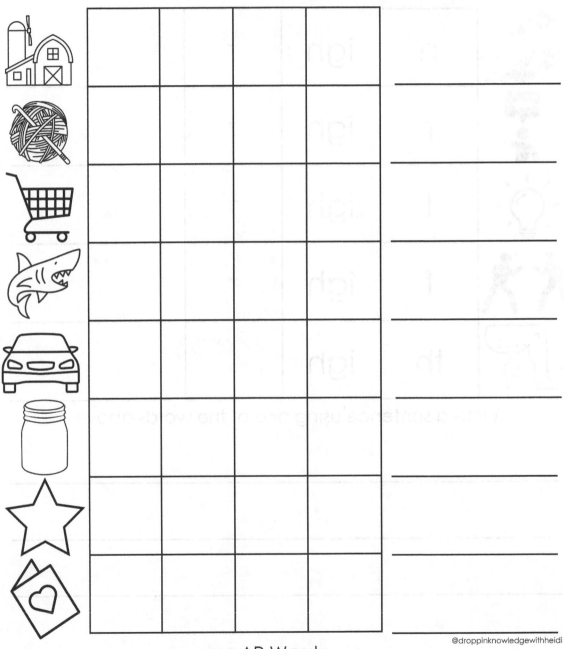

AR Words

@droppinknowledgewithheidi

ANSWER KEY

b	ar	n		
y	ar	n		
c	ar	t		
sh	ar	k		
c	ar			
j	ar			
s	t	ar		
c	ar	d		

AR Words

Say it, Map it, Write it, and Read it!

				_____
				_____
				_____
				_____
				_____
				_____
				_____
				_____

OR Words

ANSWER KEY

h	or	n	
n	or	th	
c	or	n	
s	t	or	k
s	t	or	m
h	or	se	
t	or	ch	
f	or	k	

OR Words

Say it, Map it, Write it, and Read it!

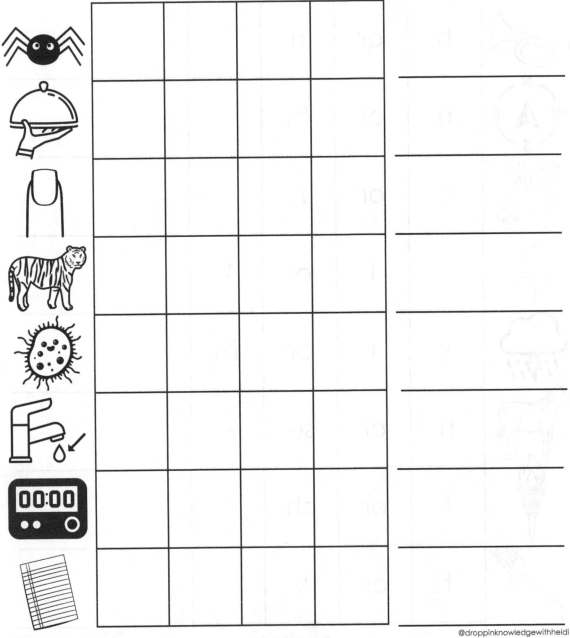

ER Words

ANSWER KEY

s	p	i	d	er
s	er	ve		
f	i	ng	er	
t	i	g	er	
g	er	m		
w	a	t	er	
t	i	m	er	
p	a	p	er	

ER Words

@droppinknowledgewithheidi

Say it, Map it,
Write it, and Read it!

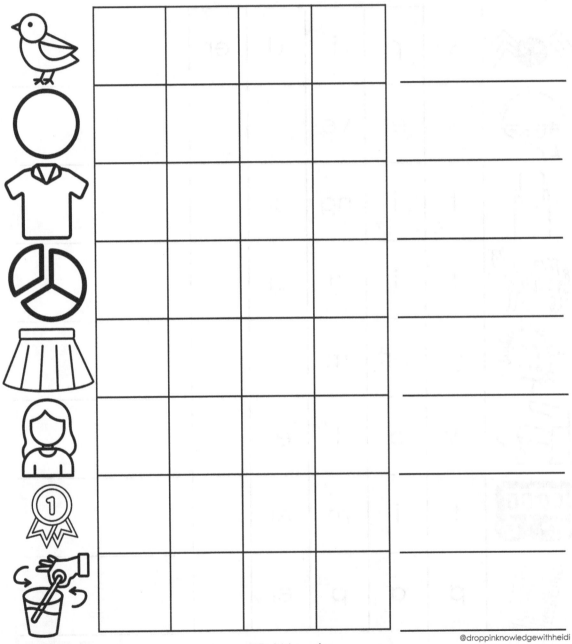

IR Words

ANSWER KEY

b	ir	d	
c	ir	c	le
sh	ir	t	
th	ir	d	
s	k	ir	t
g	ir	l	
f	ir	s	t
s	t	ir	

IR Words

@droppinknowledgewithheidi

Say it, Map it,
Write it, and Read it!

UR Words

@droppinknowledgewithheidi

ANSWER KEY

s	ur	f		
h	ur	t		
t	ur	t	le	
b	ur	g	er	
t	ur	n		
p	ur	se		
ch	ur	ch		
n	ur	se		

UR Words

Say it, Map it, Write it, and Read it!

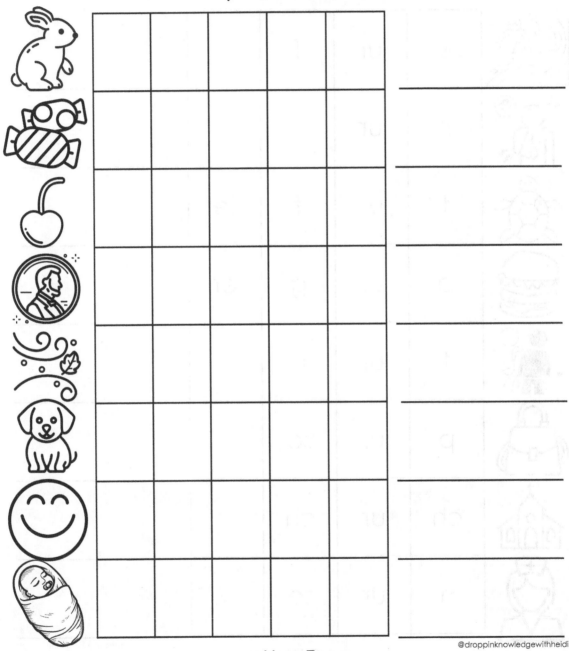

Y as E

@droppinknowledgewithheidi

ANSWER KEY

b	u	nn	y	
c	a	n	d	y
ch	e	rr	y	
p	e	nn	y	
w	i	n	d	y
p	u	pp	y	
h	a	pp	y	
b	a	b	y	

Y as E

@droppinknowledgewithheidi

Say it, Map it, Write it, and Read it!

_____

_____

_____

_____

_____

Write a sentence using one of the words above.

_____

_____

_____

Y as I

ANSWER KEY

s	p	y	
c	r	y	
f	l	y	
d	r	y	
s	k	y	

Write a sentence using one of the words above.

_____

_____

_____

Y as I

Say it, Map it, Write it, and Read it!

Vowel Digraph - Long OO

@droppinknowledgewithheidi

ANSWER KEY

m	oo	n	
s	t	oo	l
s	p	oo	n
p	oo	l	
t	oo	th	
t	oo	l	
r	oo	f	
z	oo		

Vowel Digraph - Long OO

@droppinknowledgewithheidi

Say it, Map it, Write it, and Read it!

Vowel Digraph - Short OO

ANSWER KEY

b	oo	k	
f	oo	t	
h	oo	k	
c	oo	k	ie
h	oo	d	
l	oo	k	
w	oo	d	
h	oo	f	

Vowel Digraph - Short OO

@droppinknowledgewithheidi

Say it, Map it, Write it, and Read it!

Vowel Digraph AW

ANSWER KEY

s	t	r	aw	
h	aw	k		
y	aw	n		
p	aw			
c	l	aw		
s	aw			
d	r	aw		
sh	aw	l		

Vowel Digraph AW

@droppinknowledgewithheidi

Say it, Map it,
Write it, and Read it!

				_____
				_____
				_____
				_____
				_____
				_____
				_____
				_____

Diphthong OW

ANSWER KEY

c	l	ow	n
c	r	ow	n
ow	l		
c	ow		
f	r	ow	n
d	ow	n	
g	ow	n	
c	r	ow	d

Diphthong OW

@droppinknowledgewithheidi

Say it, Map it,
Write it, and Read it!

Diphthong OU

@droppinknowledgewithheidi

ANSWER KEY

m	ou	se	
c	ou	ch	
s	ou	th	
h	ou	se	
m	ou	th	
c	ou	n	t
b	ou	n	ce
l	ou	d	

Diphthong OU

@droppinknowledgewithheidi

Droppin' Knowledge on Sight Words and Word Mapping 107

Name:_____

Let's Practice!

Say it! **the**

Count the sounds
1 2 3

Spell the sounds

Color the sounds

the

Write the word

_ _ _ _ _ _ _ _ _

Read & Highlight

1. The cat sat.

2. Pat had the map.

3. The rat ran.

4. Sam can tap the pan.

CHALLENGE: Use the word and make your own sentence!

_____

_____

Name:_____

 said

Let's Practice!

Say it!

 **said**

Count the sounds

(1) (2) (3)

Spell the sounds

Color the sounds

said

Write the word

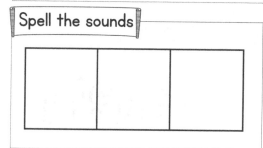 said

_____

– – – – – – – – –

_____

Read & Highlight

1. Ed said, "Get the pan."

2. "I can tap," said Pam.

3. Ted said, "I am mad!"

4. "Dad can help," said Sam.

CHALLENGE: Use the word and make your own sentence!

_____

_____

_____

Name:_____  been

Let's Practice!

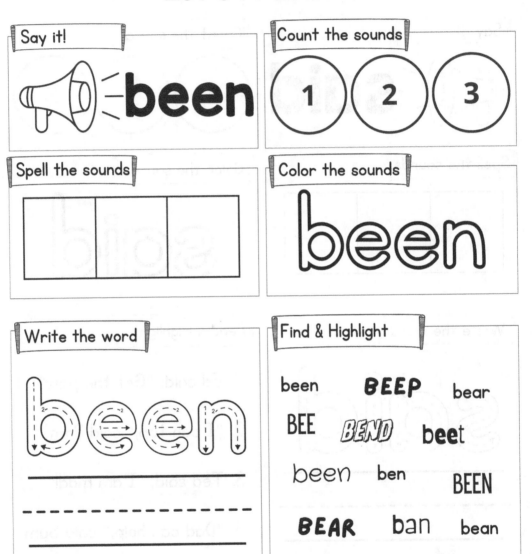

Say it!

been

Count the sounds

1 2 3

Spell the sounds

Color the sounds

been

Write the word

been

_____

- - - - - - - - - - -

_____

Find & Highlight

been   *BEEP*   bear

BEE   *BEND*   beet

been   ben   BEEN

BEAR   ban   bean

CHALLENGE: Use the word and make your own sentence!

_____

_____

_____

Name:_____

Let's Practice!

Say it!

to

Count the sounds

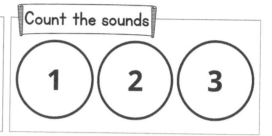

Spell the sounds

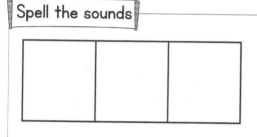

Color the sounds

Write the word

_____

- - - - - - - - - - - - - -

_____

Read & Highlight

1. Tim went to bed.

2. Pam gets to tap.

3. Kim ran to get the pan.

4. The pig went to dig.

CHALLENGE: Use the word and make your own sentence!

_____

_____

Name:_____ 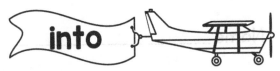 **into**

Let's Practice!

Say it!

 **into**

Count the sounds

(1) (2) (3) (4)

Spell the sounds

Color the sounds

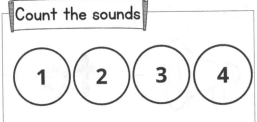 into

Write the word

_____

- - - - - - - - - - - -

_____

Read & Highlight

1. The hen went into the

   den to get fed.

2. Pat can fit into the

   red bin.

CHALLENGE: Use the word and make your own sentence!

_____

_____

_____

Name: _____

want

Let's Practice!

Say it!

want

Count the sounds

(1) (2) (3) (4)

Spell the sounds

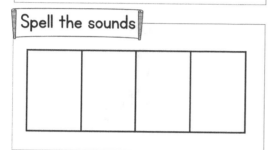

Color the sounds

want

Write the word

Read & Highlight

1. "I want to get ten red pots," said Tam.

2. Mom wants to jog.

3. The dog wants to dig.

CHALLENGE: Use the word and make your own sentence!

_____

- - - - - - - - - - - - - -

_____

Name:_____ 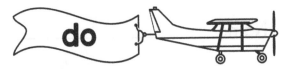 do

Let's Practice!

Say it!

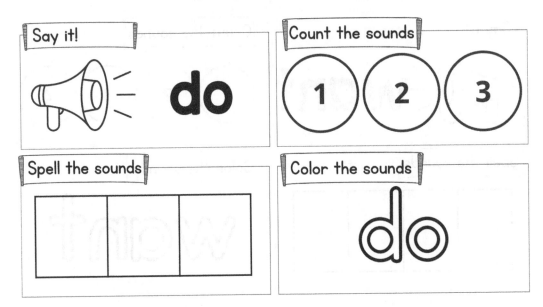 do

Count the sounds

1   2   3

Spell the sounds

Color the sounds

do

Write the word

_____

- - - - - - - - -

_____

Read & Highlight

1. Cam can do it.

2. Tom can not do it.

3. "Do not get on the

box," said Bob.

CHALLENGE: Use the word and make your own sentence!

_____

_____

Name:_____

Let's Practice!

Say it!

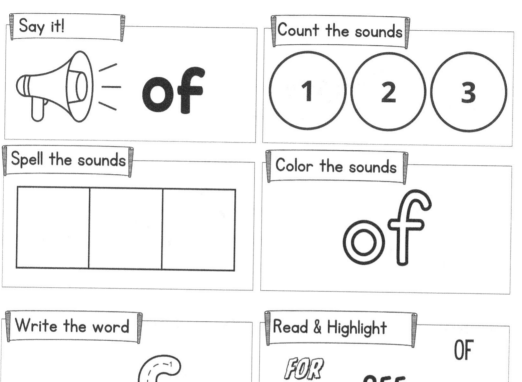 **of**

Count the sounds

(1) (2) (3)

Spell the sounds

Color the sounds

of

Write the word

_____

- - - - - - - - - - -

_____

Read & Highlight

OF

FOR

OFF

on

OF

UP

fo

ok   of

TO

FOR   of   off

CHALLENGE: Use the word and make your own sentence!

_____

_____

Name:_____

Let's Practice!

Say it!

Count the sounds

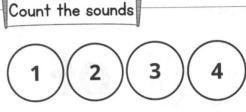

Spell the sounds

Color the sounds

from

Write the word

Read & Highlight

1. "Get the red hat from

Dad," said Mom.

2. Pam got the big pan

from Cam.

CHALLENGE: Use the word and make your own sentence!

_____

_____

Name:_____  little

Let's Practice!

Say it!

 **little**

Count the sounds

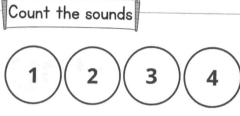
1   2   3   4

Spell the sounds

Color the sounds

Write the word

_____

- - - - - - - - - - -

_____

Read & Highlight

1. The little cat sat.

2. A little bug went into

   the web.

3. The little pig can dig.

CHALLENGE: Use the word and make your own sentence!

_____

_____

Name:_____

Let's Practice!

Say it!

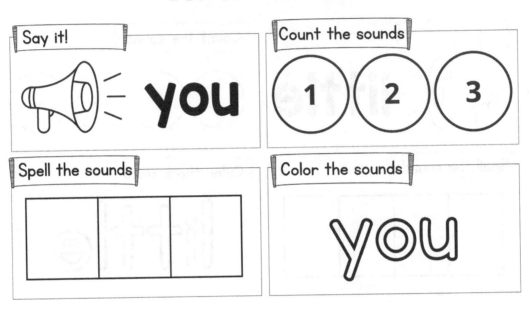

you

Count the sounds

1   2   3

Spell the sounds

Color the sounds

you

Write the word

_____

- - - - - - - - - -

_____

Read & Highlight

1. Did you get the kit?

2. Jim can help you.

3. "You can sit in the

sun," said Fran.

CHALLENGE: Use the word and make your own sentence!

_____

- -

_____

Name:_____

Let's Practice!

Say it!

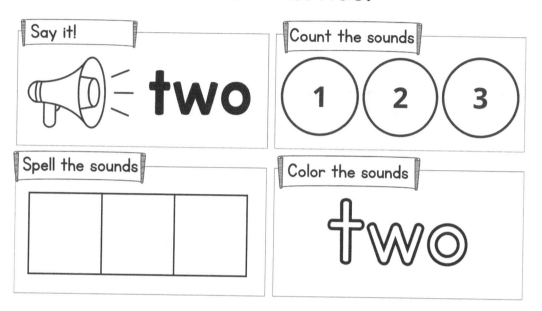 two

Count the sounds

(1) (2) (3)

Spell the sounds

Color the sounds

two

Write the word

_____

- - - - - - - - - -

_____

Read & Highlight

1. He wants two cups.

2. Mom can get two pots.

3. Two cats sat on the

rug.

CHALLENGE: Use the word and make your own sentence!

_____

_____

Name:_____  should

Let's Practice!

Say it!

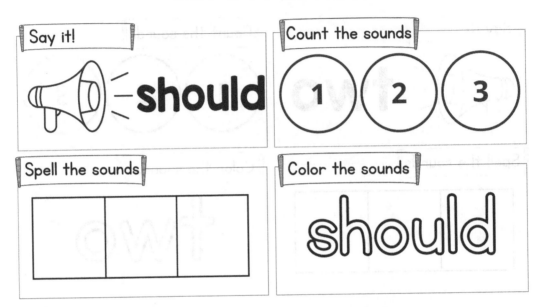 should

Count the sounds

1 2 3

Spell the sounds

Color the sounds

should

Write the word

 should

_____
- - - - - - - - - -
_____

Read & Highlight

1. She should go with you.

2. Should he help?

3. You should get two.

4. The pot should be hot.

CHALLENGE: Use the word and make your own sentence!
_____
_____
_____

Name:_____

Let's Practice!

Say it!

Count the sounds
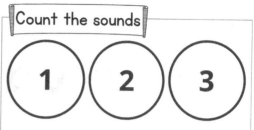

Spell the sounds

Color the sounds

could

Write the word

_____

- - - - - - - - -

_____

Read & Highlight

1. He could cut the sub.

2. The bus could go fast.

3. Could you get that?

4. Ed could get two bats.

CHALLENGE: Use the word and make your own sentence!

_____

_____

Name:_____

Let's Practice!

Say it!

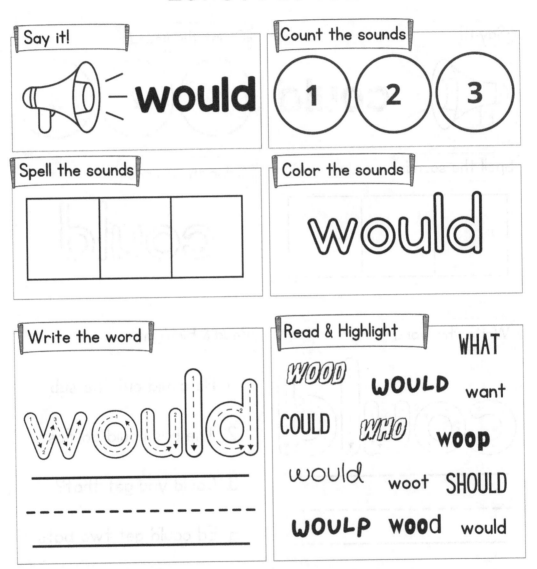

would

Count the sounds

1   2   3

Spell the sounds

Color the sounds

would

Write the word

would
_____
- - - - - - - - - - - -
_____

Read & Highlight

WHAT

WOOD   WOULD   want

COULD   WHO   woop

would   woot   SHOULD

WOULP   wood   would

CHALLENGE: Use the word and make your own sentence!
_____
- -
_____

Name:_____

Let's Practice!

Say it!

Count the sounds

(1) (2) (3)

Spell the sounds

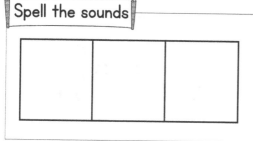

Color the sounds

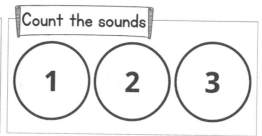

who

Write the word

Read & Highlight

1. Who did that?

2. Who got the pen?

3. Who said no?

4. Who went to bed?

CHALLENGE: Use the word and make your own sentence!

_____

_____

Name:_____

Let's Practice!

Say it!

Count the sounds

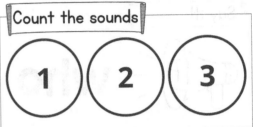

Spell the sounds

Color the sounds

Write the word

Read & Highlight

1. Can you wash this?

2. "I want you to wash

   this dish," said Hal.

3. She can wash the dog.

CHALLENGE: Use the word and make your own sentence!

_____

_____

Name:_____

Let's Practice!

Say it!

Count the sounds
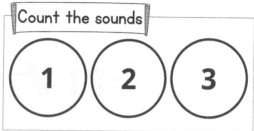

Spell the sounds
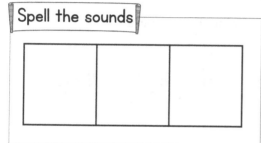

Color the sounds

Write the word

Read & Highlight

1. What did the fox do?

2. What can you do?

3. What did you win?

4. What do you want?

CHALLENGE: Use the word and make your own sentence!

_____

_____

Name:_____  laugh

Let's Practice!

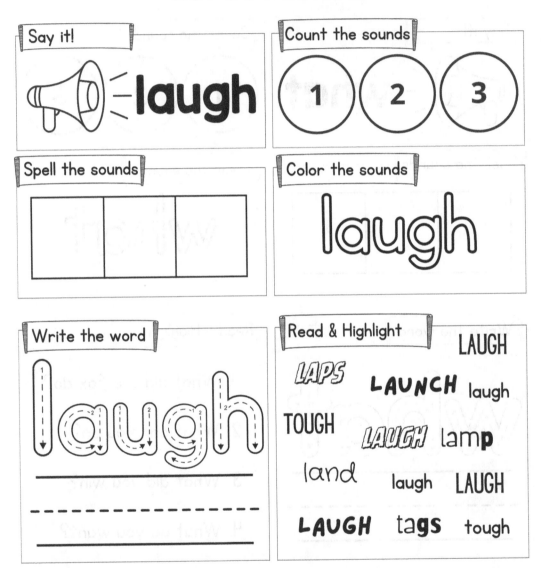

Say it!

laugh

Count the sounds

1   2   3

Spell the sounds

Color the sounds

laugh

Write the word

laugh
_____
_ _ _ _ _ _ _ _ _
_____

Read & Highlight

LAUGH
LAPS   LAUNCH   laugh
TOUGH   LAUGH   lamp
land   laugh   LAUGH
LAUGH   tags   tough

CHALLENGE: Use the word and make your own sentence!
_____
_____
_____

Name:_____

Let's Practice!

Say it!

Count the sounds
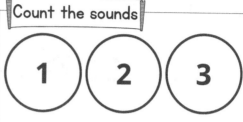

Spell the sounds

Color the sounds
some

Write the word
some
_____
- - - - - - - - - -
_____

Read & Highlight

1. She can bring some

   hats to the hut.

2. Ming got some chips

   and sat on the rug.

CHALLENGE: Use the word and make your own sentence!
_____
_____

Name:_____  come

Let's Practice!

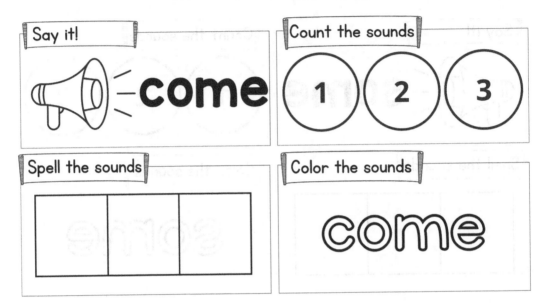

Say it!

come

Count the sounds

1   2   3

Spell the sounds

Color the sounds

come

Write the word

come

_____
- - - - - - - - - - - - - -
_____

Read & Highlight

1. Come with us and get

on the bus.

2. He could come to the

shop.

CHALLENGE: Use the word and make your own sentence!
_____
_____
_____

Name:_____

Let's Practice!

Say it!

put

Count the sounds

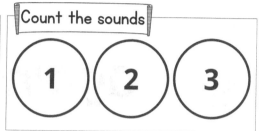

(1) (2) (3)

Spell the sounds

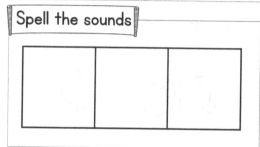

Color the sounds

put

Write the word

put

_____

- - - - - - - - - - - -

_____

Read & Highlight

1. Tish will put the fish in the dish.

2. Can you put that in the trash?

CHALLENGE: Use the word and make your own sentence!

_____

_____

Name:_____

Let's Practice!

Say it!

Count the sounds

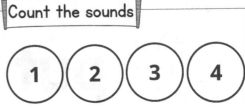

Spell the sounds

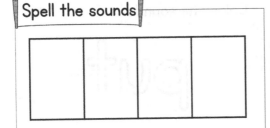

Color the sounds

Write the word

Read & Highlight

1. We will go to that

   shop again.

2. Can you tell me again?

3. Let's do that again!

CHALLENGE: Use the word and make your own sentence!

_____

_____

Name:_____

Let's Practice!

Say it!

done

Count the sounds

1 2 3

Spell the sounds

Color the sounds

done

Write the word

done
_____
- - - - - - - - - - -
_____

Read & Highlight

DONE   DON'T

DOTS   none

DON   TONE   done

don't   done   BONE

DONE   dots   lone

CHALLENGE: Use the word and make your own sentence!
_____
_____

Name:_____

Let's Practice!

Say it!

 **does**

Count the sounds

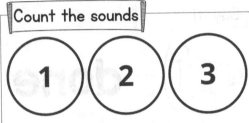

1   2   3

Spell the sounds

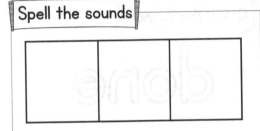

Color the sounds

does

Write the word

_ _ _ _ _ _ _ _ _

Read & Highlight

1. Does she want to go

on the big ship?

2. What does that clock

do?

CHALLENGE: Use the word and make your own sentence!

Name:_____

Let's Practice!

Say it!

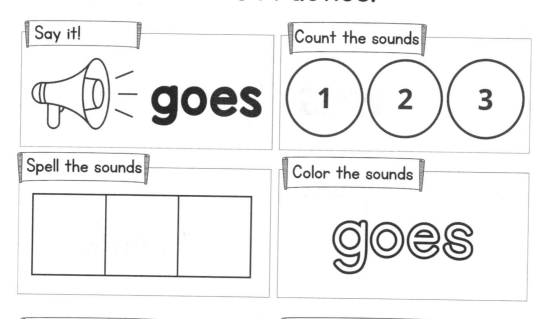

goes

Count the sounds

1 2 3

Spell the sounds

Color the sounds

goes

Write the word

Read & Highlight

1. His truck goes fast in the mud.

2. That cat goes to bed at six.

CHALLENGE: Use the word and make your own sentence!

Name:_____ 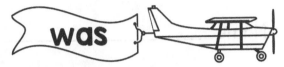 **was**

Let's Practice!

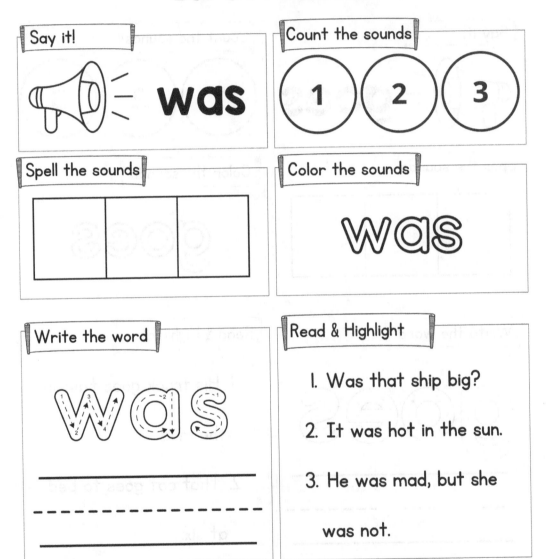

Say it!

was

Count the sounds

1   2   3

Spell the sounds

Color the sounds

was

Write the word

was

_____

— — — — — — —

_____

Read & Highlight

1. Was that ship big?

2. It was hot in the sun.

3. He was mad, but she

   was not.

CHALLENGE: Use the word and make your own sentence!

_____

_____

_____

Name:_____  write

Let's Practice!

Say it!

 write

Count the sounds

(1) (2) (3)

Spell the sounds

Color the sounds

write

Write the word

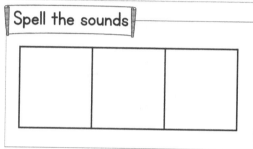 write

_____

- - - - - - - - - - - -

_____

Read & Highlight

1. Can you write a note?

2. We will write the date.

3. The man can write

   with the black pen.

CHALLENGE: Use the word and make your own sentence!

_____

_____

_____

Name:_____  **one**

Let's Practice!

Say it!

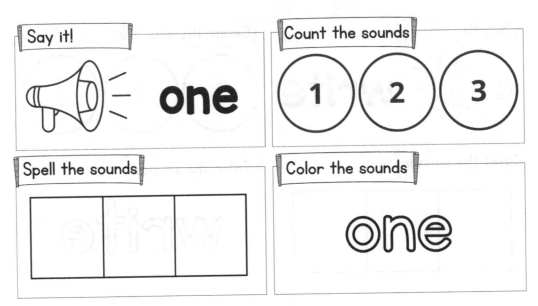

one

Count the sounds

(1) (2) (3)

Spell the sounds

Color the sounds

one

Write the word

one

_____

- - - - - - - -

_____

Read & Highlight

1. This is the red one.

2. She will get one lime.

3. One fish was pink.

4. This one is the best!

CHALLENGE: Use the word and make your own sentence!

_____

_____

_____

Name:_____  **once**

Let's Practice!

Say it!

🔊 **once**

Count the sounds

(1) (2) (3) (4)

Spell the sounds

Color the sounds

once

Write the word

once

_____

- - - - - - - - - - - - - - -

_____

Read & Highlight

ONCE

ONE   ONTO   cone

ONCE   DANCE   once

once   one   ONTO

CONE   once   dance

CHALLENGE: Use the word and make your own sentence!

_____

_____

Name:_____

seven

Let's Practice!

Say it!

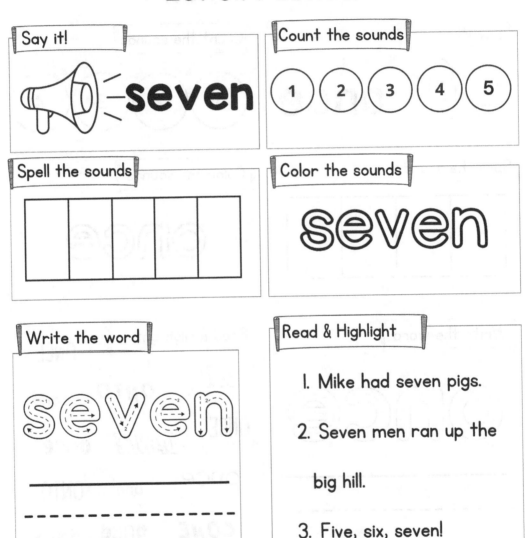

seven

Count the sounds

(1) (2) (3) (4) (5)

Spell the sounds

Color the sounds

seven

Write the word

seven

_____

- - - - - - - -

_____

Read & Highlight

1. Mike had seven pigs.

2. Seven men ran up the

   big hill.

3. Five, six, seven!

CHALLENGE: Use the word and make your own sentence!

_____

_____

_____

Name:_____

they

Let's Practice!

Say it!

they

Count the sounds

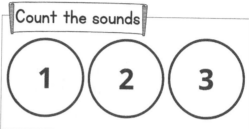
1 2 3

Spell the sounds

Color the sounds

they

Write the word

they

_____

- - - - - - - -

_____

Read & Highlight

1. They can drive fast.

2. Will they win the race?

3. Can they get into the cab?

CHALLENGE: Use the word and make your own sentence!

_____

_____

Name:_____  today

Let's Practice!

Say it!

 today

Count the sounds

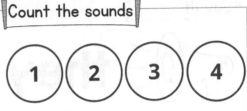
1 2 3 4

Spell the sounds

Color the sounds

today

Write the word

 today

_____

- - - - - - - - - - -

_____

Read & Highlight

1. Kate will write a note today.

2. Today he will drive to the shop.

CHALLENGE: Use the word and make your own sentence!

_____

_____

Name:_____

Let's Practice!

know

Say it!

Count the sounds

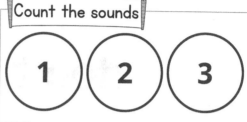

Spell the sounds

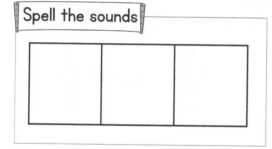

Color the sounds

Write the word

know

_____

- - - - - - - - - -

_____

Read & Highlight

1. Did you know that one

plus one is two?

2. I know the duck likes

to swim in the pond.

CHALLENGE: Use the word and make your own sentence!

_____

_____

Name:_____

Let's Practice!

Say it!

Count the sounds

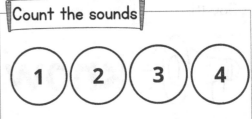

Spell the sounds

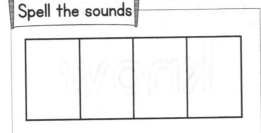

Color the sounds

Write the word

_____

- - - - - - - - - - - - - -

_____

Read & Highlight

1. Dad said, "Don't take the last slice of cake."

2. Don't drive up that big hill.

CHALLENGE: Use the word and make your own sentence!

_____

_____

Name:_____

Let's Practice!

eight

Say it!

 **eight**

Count the sounds

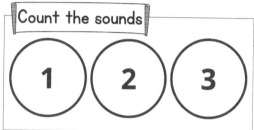
1   2   3

Spell the sounds

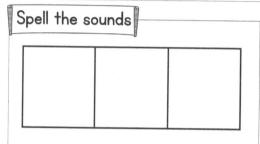

Color the sounds

 eight

Write the word

_____

— — — — — — —

_____

Read & Highlight

1. The cat had eight mice.

2. Six, seven, eight!

3. She got eight yellow

beads at the shop.

CHALLENGE: Use the word and make your own sentence!

_____

_____

Name:_____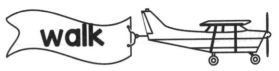

Let's Practice!

Say it!

Count the sounds

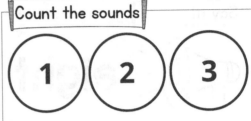

Spell the sounds

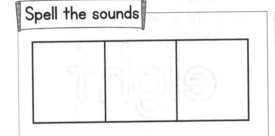

Color the sounds

Write the word

_____

- - - - - - - - - - - - -

_____

Read & Highlight

1. The queen likes to walk at night.

2. We can walk fast.

3. Can you walk like this?

CHALLENGE: Use the word and make your own sentence!

_____

_____

_____

Name:_____

Let's Practice!

Say it!

are

Count the sounds

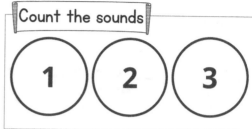

1 2 3

Spell the sounds

Color the sounds

are

Write the word

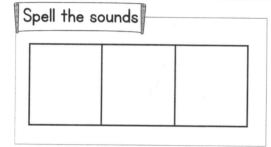

are

_____

- - - - - - - - - - -

_____

Read & Highlight

1. "Are you going to get

   that car?" asked Jack.

2. We are done.

3. Are you going to run?

CHALLENGE: Use the word and make your own sentence!

_____

_____

Name:_____  carry

Let's Practice!

Say it!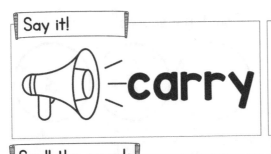

Count the sounds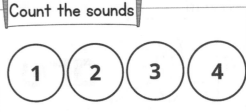

Spell the sounds

Color the sounds

carry

Write the word

Read & Highlight

1. Let's help Pete carry the big boxes.

2. Can you carry that gift to the car?

CHALLENGE: Use the word and make your own sentence!

_____

_____

Name:_____

Let's Practice!

Say it!

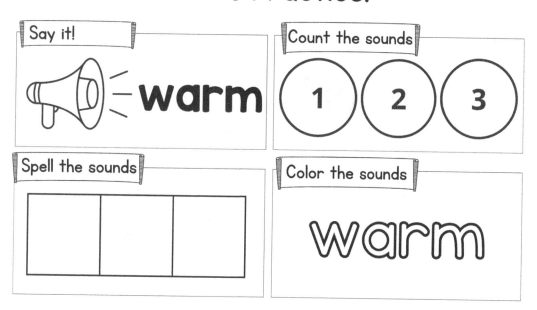
warm

Count the sounds

(1) (2) (3)

Spell the sounds

Color the sounds

warm

Write the word

_____

- - - - - - - - - - -

_____

Read & Highlight

1. It is a warm day.

2. This will keep the

   beans warm.

3. Come in to warm up!

CHALLENGE: Use the word and make your own sentence!

_____

_____

_____

Name:_____ 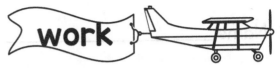 work

Let's Practice!

Say it!

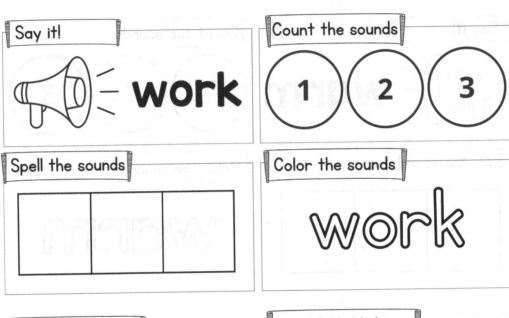 work

Count the sounds

1 2 3

Spell the sounds

Color the sounds

work

Write the word

work

_____

- - - - - - - - - - -

_____

Read & Highlight

1. He has to go to work

   at eight.

2. Did you do your

   homework?

CHALLENGE: Use the word and make your own sentence!

_____

_____

_____

Name:_____

Let's Practice!

Say it!

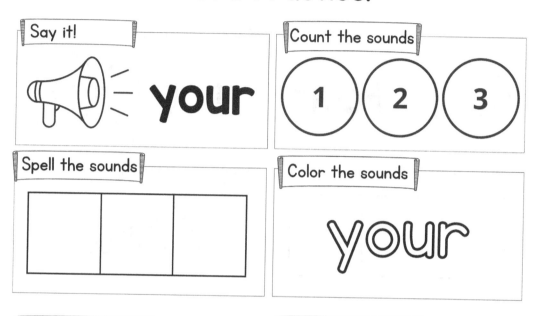

your

Count the sounds

(1) (2) (3)

Spell the sounds

Color the sounds

your

Write the word

your

_____

- - - - - - - - - - -

_____

Read & Highlight

1. Is that your sister?

2. Your shirt is nice.

3. Can you get your

   backpack so we can go?

CHALLENGE: Use the word and make your own sentence!

_____

_____

_____

Name:_____

Let's Practice!

Say it!

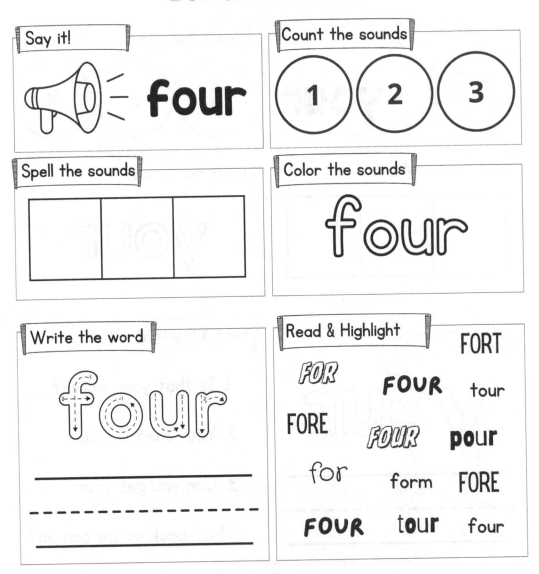

four

Count the sounds

1 2 3

Spell the sounds

Color the sounds

four

Write the word

four

_ _ _ _ _ _ _ _

Read & Highlight

FOR FOUR FORT tour

FORE FOUR pour

for form FORE

FOUR tour four

CHALLENGE: Use the word and make your own sentence!

Name:_____

Let's Practice!

Say it!

very

Count the sounds
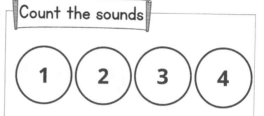
1 2 3 4

Spell the sounds
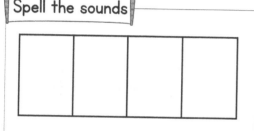

Color the sounds
very

Write the word

very

Read & Highlight

1. Her scarf is very nice.

2. The math work was

   very hard.

3. It is very hot.

CHALLENGE: Use the word and make your own sentence!
_____
_____
_____

Name:_____

Let's Practice!

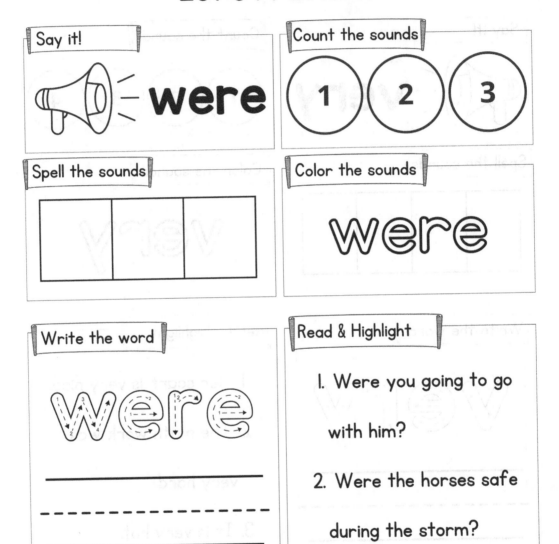

Say it!

were

Count the sounds

1 2 3

Spell the sounds

Color the sounds

were

Write the word

were

_____

- - - - - - - -

_____

Read & Highlight

1. Were you going to go

with him?

2. Were the horses safe

during the storm?

CHALLENGE: Use the word and make your own sentence!

_____

_____

Name:_____

Let's Practice!

Say it!

 **together**

Count the sounds

(1) (2) (3) (4) (5) (6)

Spell the sounds

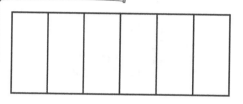

Color the sounds

together

Write the word

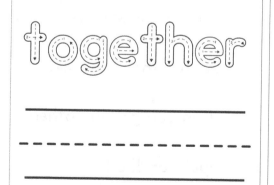

_____

– – – – – – – – –

_____

Read & Highlight

1. Can we get together

   on your birthday?

2. Let's work on math

   together.

CHALLENGE: Use the word and make your own sentence!

_____

- - - - - - - - - - - - - - - - - - - -

_____

Name:_____

Let's Practice!

Say it!

 **other**

Count the sounds

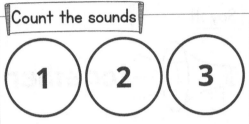

Spell the sounds

Color the sounds

other

Write the word

other

_____

- - - - - - - - - - - -

_____

Read & Highlight

1. The other song is

   better than this one.

2. Can you get the other

   quilt for the bed?

CHALLENGE: Use the word and make your own sentence!

_____

- -

_____

Name:_____

Let's Practice!

Say it!

Count the sounds

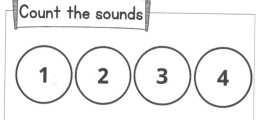

Spell the sounds

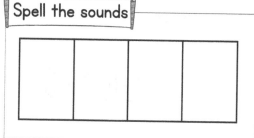

Color the sounds

every

Write the word

_____

- - - - - - - - - - -

_____

Read & Highlight

1. We go to that place

every year in March.

2. Every tree has a

branch.

CHALLENGE: Use the word and make your own sentence!

_____

_____

Name:_____

Let's Practice!

Say it!

Count the sounds

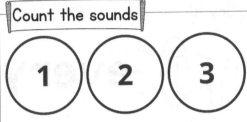

Spell the sounds

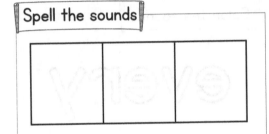

Color the sounds

there

Write the word

_____

_ _ _ _ _ _ _ _ _ _ _

_____

Read & Highlight

1. There is a red frog in the tree.

2. I have been there before.

CHALLENGE: Use the word and make your own sentence!

_____

_ _

_____

Name:_____

Let's Practice!

Say it!

Count the sounds

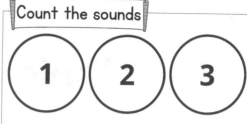

Spell the sounds

Color the sounds

where

Write the word

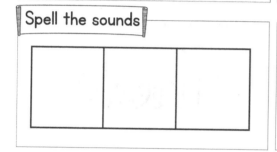

_____

- - - - - - - - - - - - - - -

_____

Read & Highlight

1. Where does the sun go

   at night?

2. Do you know where

   the cat went?

CHALLENGE: Use the word and make your own sentence!

_____

_____

Name:_____  their

Let's Practice!

 their

Count the sounds

(1) (2) (3)

Spell the sounds

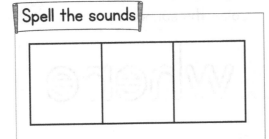

Color the sounds

Write the word

their

_____

- - - - - - - - - - - - -

_____

Read & Highlight

1. We went to their

   farm to see the goats.

2. Their truck is bigger

   than mine.

CHALLENGE: Use the word and make your own sentence!

_____

_____

Name:_____

Let's Practice!

Say it!

Count the sounds

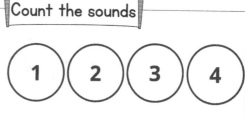

Spell the sounds

Color the sounds

many

Write the word

_____

- - - - - - - - - - -

_____

Read & Highlight

1. There are many leaves

on the tree.

2. We have so many cats.

3. Many kids like candy.

CHALLENGE: Use the word and make your own sentence!
_____

....

_____

Name:_____

any

Let's Practice!

Say it!

any

Count the sounds

1　2　3

Spell the sounds

Color the sounds

any

Write the word

any

_____

- - - - - - - - - - -

_____

Read & Highlight

1. Do you have any cash?

2. Are there any sheep

   on the farm?

3. Do we have any cake?

CHALLENGE: Use the word and make your own sentence!

_____

_____

Name:_____

Let's Practice!

Say it!

pretty

Count the sounds

(1) (2) (3) (4) (5)

Spell the sounds

Color the sounds

pretty

Write the word

_____

- - - - - - - - - - -

_____

Read & Highlight

1. The sunset is pretty.

2. The park was pretty fun!

3. That is a pretty shirt.

CHALLENGE: Use the word and make your own sentence!

_____

_____

_____

Name:_____  **buy**

Let's Practice!

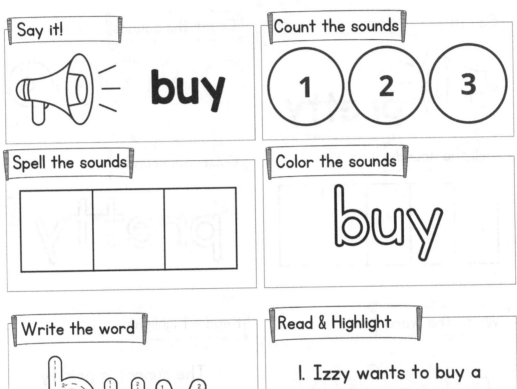

Say it!

buy

Count the sounds

1 2 3

Spell the sounds

Color the sounds

buy

Write the word

buy

_____

- - - - - - - - - -

Read & Highlight

1. Izzy wants to buy a

doll at the store.

2. Can you buy this game

for me?

CHALLENGE: Use the word and make your own sentence!

_____

_____

Name:_____

Let's Practice!

Say it!

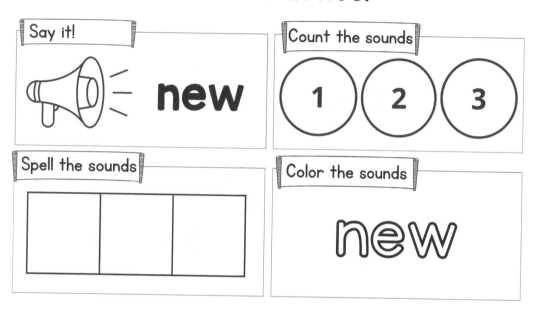

new

Count the sounds

1 2 3

Spell the sounds

Color the sounds

new

Write the word

_____

— — — — — — —

_____

Read & Highlight

1. The new game is too

hard.

2. Do you want to go get

a new truck?

CHALLENGE: Use the word and make your own sentence!

_____

_____

_____

Name:_____

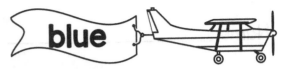

Let's Practice!

Say it!

blue

Count the sounds

1 2 3

Spell the sounds

Color the sounds

blue

Write the word

blue

_____

_ _ _ _ _ _ _ _ _ _

_____

Read & Highlight

BLUE
BLACK BLOW blur
BLUE BUMP blue
blume burp BLACK
BLUE plue blue

CHALLENGE: Use the word and make your own sentence!

_____

_____

_____

Name:_____  because

Let's Practice!

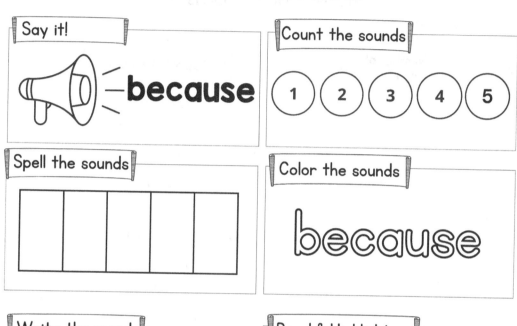

Say it!

because

Count the sounds

(1) (2) (3) (4) (5)

Spell the sounds

Color the sounds

because

Write the word

because
_____
- - - - - - - -
_____

Read & Highlight

1. The shark ate the fish

because it was hungry.

2. She put on a hat and

gloves because it is cold.

CHALLENGE: Use the word and make your own sentence!

_____
_____

Unit 1

This cheat sheet will help you know how words are mapped and what do to when teaching words with an irregular sound spelling.

Word	Number of Sounds	Sounds to Spell
at	2	/ă/ and /t/
and	3	/ă/, /n/, /d/
an	2	/ă/ and /n/
can	3	/c/, /ă/, /n/
am	3	/ă/ and /m/
had	3	/h/ /ă/ /d/
ask	3	/ă/, /s/, /k/
ran	3	/r/, /ă/, /n/
fast	4	/f/, /ă/, /s/, /t/
the	**2**	You can choose to teach TH here or let kids know this is something they will learn soon. If you choose to wait, mark this part with a star and we will remove the star once kids have learned this digraph. **Say, "How do we normally spell /ŭ/? Yes, usually with a U, but In this word, we spell /ŭ/ with an e. Let's circle it so we remember that spelling."**
get	3	/g/, /ĕ/, /t/
red	3	/r/, /ĕ/, /d/
yes	3	/y/, /ĕ/, /s/
ten	3	/t/, /ĕ/, /n/
went	4	/w/, /ĕ/, /n/, /t/
let	3	/l/, /ĕ/, /t/
help	4	/h/, /ĕ/, /l/, /p/
best	4	/b/, /ĕ/, /s/, /t/

Word	Number of Sounds	Sounds to Spell
said	3	/s/ is spelled with an s. **Say, "How do we normally spell /ĕ/? Yes, usually we spell it with an e but in this word, we spell it with ai. Let's circle it so we remember that spelling."** /d/ is spelled with a d.
been	3	/b/ is spelled with a b. **Say, "How do we normally spell /ĕ/? Yes, usually we spell it with one e but in this word, we spell it with two e's. Let's circle it so we remember that spelling."** /n/ is spelled with an n.
it	2	/ĭ/ and /t/
in	2	/ĭ/ and /n/
if	2	/ĭ/ and /f/
its	3	/ĭ/, /t/, /s/
big	3	/b/, /ĭ/, /g/
did	3	/d/, /ĭ/, /d/
sit	3	/s/, /ĭ/, /t/
him	3	/h/, /ĭ/, /m/
six	4	/s/, /ĭ/, /k/, /s/
to	2	/t/ is spelled with a t. **We have not taught /oo/ yet so let kids know that in this word, we are going to spell /oo/ with an o. Say, "Let's circle it so we remember the spelling."**
into	4	/ĭ/ is spelled with an i. /n/ is spelled with an n. /t/ is spelled with a t. **We have not taught /oo/ yet so let kids know that in this word, we are going to spell /oo/ with an o. Say, "Let's circle it so we remember the spelling."**
on	2	/ŏ/ and /n/
not	3	/n/, /ŏ/, /t/
hot	3	/h/, /ŏ/, /t/
got	3	/g/, /ŏ/, /t/

Word	Number of Sounds	Sounds to Spell
off	2	/ŏ/ and /f/ - *let kids know that sometimes /f/ is spelled with two f's
stop	4	/s/, /t/, /ŏ/, /p/
mom	3	/m/, /ŏ/, /m/
want	4	/w/ is spelled with a w. Say, "How do we normally spell /ŏ/? Yes, usually we spell it with an o but in this word, we spell it with an a. Let's circle it so we remember that spelling." /n/ is spelled with an n. /t/ is spelled with a t.
do	2	/d/ is spelled with a d. We have not taught /oo/ yet so let kids know that in this word, we are going to spell /oo/ with an o. Say, "Let's circle it so we remember the spelling."
up	2	/ŭ/ and /p/
us	2	/ŭ/ and /s/
cut	3	/k/, /ŭ/, /t/
run	3	/r/, /ŭ/, /n/
but	3	/b/, /ŭ/, /t/
jump	4	/j/, /ŭ/, /m/, /p/
just	4	/j/, /ŭ/, /s/, /t/
must	4	/m/, /ŭ/, /s/, /t/
upon	4	/ŭ/, /p/, /ŏ/, /n/
of	2	Say, "How do we normally spell /ŭ/? Yes, we usually spell it with a U, but in this word, we are going to spell it with an o. Let's circle it to remember that spelling. And how do we spell /v/? Yes, normally with a v but in this word, we spell it with an f. Let's circle it to remember that spelling."
from	4	/f/ is spelled with an f. /r/ is spelled with an r Say, "How do we normally spell /ŭ/? Yes, with a u but in this word, we are going to spell it with an o. Let's circle it so we remember that spelling." /m/ is spelled with an m.
a	1	Typically, we pronounce this word with a long A sound or a schwa. This is a good time to talk to kids about the different sounds of A as a letter and A as a word.

Word	Number of Sounds	Sounds to Spell
be	2	/b/ and /ē/
he	2	/h/ and /ē/
me	2	/m/ and /ē/
no	2	/n/ and /ō/
so	2	/s/ and /ō/
we	2	/w/ and /ē/
I	1	/ī/
go	2	/g/ and /ō/
open	4	/ō/, /p/, /ĕ/, /n/
little	4	/l/ is spelled with an l. /ĭ/ is spelled with an i. Let kids know that /t/ can be spelled with two t's. Say, "How do we normally spell /l/? Yes, usually we spell it with an l but since every syllable needs a vowel, in this word we are going to spell it with an l and an e. Let's put a star up there to remember that spelling until we learn more about syllable types."
you	2	/y/ is spelled with a y. Kids may not know how to spell /oo/ yet. Say, "In this word we are going to spell /oo/ with an o and a u. Let's circle this part so we remember that spelling."

Unit 2

This cheat sheet will help you know how words are mapped and what do to when teaching words with an irregular sound spelling.

Word	Number of Sounds	Sounds to Spell
with	3	/w/ /ĭ/ /th/
this	3	/th/ /ĭ/ /s/
that	3	/th/ /ă/ /t/
than	3	/th/ /ă/ /n/
then	3	/th/ /ĕ/ /n/
them	3	/th/ /ĕ/ /m/
both	3	/b/ /ō/ /th/
two	**2**	/t/ is spelled with a T. **Say, "How do we normally spell /oo/?"** Kids may not know this yet. **"In the word two, the /oo/ sound is spelled with a w and an o."** *Fun fact: TW is a phonestheme and can sometimes represent the number two such as in the words twin, twelve, and two!*
she	2	/sh/ /ē/
wish	3	/w/ /ĭ/ /sh/
should	**3**	/sh/ is spelled with SH. **Say, "How do we normally spell /oo/?"** Kids may not know this yet. **"In the word should, we are going to spell this sound with OUL."** /d/ is spelled with a D.
could	**3**	/k/ is spelled with a C. **Say, "How do we normally spell /oo/?"** Kids may not know this yet. **"In the word should, we are going to spell this sound with OUL."** /d/ is spelled with a D.
would	**3**	/w/ is spelled with a W. **Say, "How do we normally spell /oo/?"** Kids may not know this yet. **"In the word should, we are going to spell this sound with OUL."** /d/ is spelled with a D.
when	3	/wh/ /ĕ/ /n/

Word	Number of Sounds	Sounds to Spell
who	2	/h/ is spelled with a WH. **Say, "How do we normally spell /oo/?"** Kids may not know this yet. **"In the word who, we are going to spell this sound with an O."**
wash	3	/w/ is spelled with a W. **Say, "How do we normally spell /ŏ/? Yes, usually this is spelled with an O but in the word wash, we are going to spell this sound with an A. This is because most of the time when an A follows a W it makes this sound!"** /sh/ is spelled with a SH.
what	3	/w/ is spelled with a WH. **Say, "How do we normally spell /ŭ/? Yes, we usually spell it with a U but in the word WHAT, we are going to spell it with an A."** /t/ is spelled with a T.
which	3	/wh/ /ĭ/ /ch/
much	3	/m/ /ŭ/ /ch/
laugh	3	/l/ is spelled with an L. /ă/ is spelled with an A. **Say, How do we normally spell /f/? Yes, usually this is spelled with an F but in the word laugh, we are going to spell this sound with an –ugh."**
long	3	/l/ /ŏ/ /ng/
going	4	/g/ /ō/ /ĭ/ /ng/
sing	3	/s/ /ĭ/ /ng/
bring	4	/b/ /r/ /ĭ/ /ng/
some	3	/s/ is spelled with an S. **Say, "How do we normally spell /ŭ/? Yes, we normally spell that with a U, but in the word some, we are going to use an O."** /m/ is spelled with an M.
come	3	/k/ is spelled with a C. **Say, "How do we normally spell /ŭ/? Yes, we normally spell that with a U, but in the word come, we are going to use an O."** /m/ is spelled with an M.
well	3	/w/ /ĕ/ /l/ **"Remember the L at the end of the word is doubled because of the floss rule."**
tell	3	/t/ /ĕ/ /l/ **"Remember the L at the end of the word is doubled because of the floss rule."**
will	3	/w/ /ĭ/ /l/ **"Remember the L at the end of the word is doubled because of the floss rule."**

Word	Number of Sounds	Sounds to Spell
shall	3	/sh/ /ă/ /l/ **"Remember the L at the end of the word is doubled because of the floss rule."**
put	3	/p/ is spelled with a P. **Say, "How do we normally spell /oo/?"** Kids may not know this yet. **"In the word put, we are going to spell this sound with U."** /t/ is spelled with a T.
drink	5	/d/ /r/ /ĭ/ /ng/ /k/
thank	4	/th/ /ā/ /ng/ /k/
think	4	/th/ /ĭ/ /ng/ /k/
again	4	**Say, "How do we normally spell /ŭ/? Yes, usually this is spelled with a U but usually at the beginning of a two-syllable word this is spelled with an A."** /g/ is spelled with a G. **"Now say how do we usually spell /ī/? Correct, it is normally I, but in this word it is the –AI."** /n/ is spelled with an N
black	4	/b/ /l/ /ă/ /k/
pick	3	/p/ /ĭ/ /k/
done	3	/d/ is spelled with a D. **Say, "How do we normally spell /ŭ/? Yes, usually this is spelled with a U but in the word done we will use an O."** /n/ is spelled with an N.

Unit 3

This cheat sheet will help you know how words are mapped and what do to when teaching words with an irregular sound spelling.

Word	Number of Sounds	Sounds to Spell
as	2	/ă/ /z/
has	3	/h/ /ă/ /z/
is	2	/ĭ/ /z/
his	3	/h/ /ĭ/ /z/
does	**3**	/d/ is spelled with a D. **Say, "How do we normally spell /ŭ/? Yes, usually this is spelled with a U but in the word does we will use a –OE."** /z/ is spelled with an S.
goes	**3**	/g/ is spelled with /g/. **Say, "How do we normally spell /ō/? Yes, usually this is spelled with an O but in the word goes we will use a –OE."** /z/ is spelled with an S.
was	**3**	/w/ is spelled with a W. **Say, "How do we normally spell /ŭ/? Yes, usually this is spelled with a U but in the word was it is an A."** /z/ is spelled with an S.
use	3	/y/ /u/ /z/
ate	2	/ā/ /t/
came	3	/k/ /ā/ /m/
made	3	/m/ /ā/ /d/
make	3	/m/ /ā/ k/
take	3	/t/ /ā/ /k/
gave	3	/g/ /ā/ /v/
five	3	/f/ /ĭ/ /v/

Word	Number of Sounds	Sounds to Spell
like	3	/l/ /ī/ /k/
ride	3	/r/ /ī/ /d/
time	3	/t/ /ī/ /m/
white	3	/wh/ /ī/ /t/
here	3	/h/ //ē/ /r/
those	3	/th/ /ō/ /z/
these	3	/th/ /ē/ /z/
live	3	/l/ /i/ /v/ **or** /l/ /ī/ /v/
have	3	/h/ /ă/ /v/
give	3	/g/ /ī/ /v/
write	3	Say, "What usually spells the /r/ sound? Yes, it is usually spelled with an R, but this has a silent letter with it and we use WR, lets circle that to help us remember." /ī/ is spelled with an I and /t/ is spelled with a T.
one	3	Say, "This is a very sneaky word for us. What are the first two sounds we hear? Yes! /w/ and /u/. What usually spells the /w/ sound? Perfect, W is right and what usually spells the /u/ sound? That's right U. Though in this word O is representing the /w/ and /u/ sounds. What is the next sound we here in ONE? Yes, it is the nasal /n/, and we typically spell /n/ with a... N! But for this word it is represented with –NE, because E is not doing its right job." *
once	4	Say, "Just like the word ONE, this is another tricky word. What are the first two sounds? Yes /w/ and /u/. What did we use to represent those in the word ONE. Perfect, it is O for this word as well." /n/ is spelled with an N. Say, "What is the last sound we hear? Yes /s/, how do we usually spell that, yup with an S. In this word we will use –ce to spell that /s/ sound." *

Word	Number of Sounds	Sounds to Spell
see	2	/s/ /ē/
green	4	/g/ /r/ /ē/ /n/
keep	3	/k/ /ē/ /p/
sleep	4	/s/ /l/ //ē/ /p/
three	3	/th/ /r/ /ē/
seven	5	/s/ is spelled with an S. /ĕ/ is spelled with an E. /v/ is spelled with a V. **Say, "What is the next sound we hear? Yes, /ĭ/ and how do we usually spell that? Perfect, with an I, in this word we are going to use another E."** /n/ is spelled with an N.
eat	2	/ē/ /t/
read	3	/r/ /ē/ /d/ or /r/ /ĕ/ /d/ **
clean	4	/k/ /l/ /ē/ /n/
each	2	/ē/ /ch/
please	4	/p/ /l/ /ē/ /z/
say	2	/s/ /ā/
play	3	/p/ /l/ /ā/
way	2	/w/ /ā/
day	2	/d/ /ā/
may	2	/m/ /ā/

Word	Number of Sounds	Sounds to Spell
away	3	Say, "That first sound is...? Yes, /u/, how do we usually spell that? Yes with a U. Though in this word we will use an A." /w/ is spelled with a W and /ā/ is spelled with the Vowel Team -AY
they	2	/th/ is spelled with digraph TH. Say, "What's the last sound we hear? Perfect, /ā/, how have we been spelling that Vowel Team? Yes -AY, in this word though we will use -EY."
today	4	/t/ is spelled with a T. Say, "What's the next sound we hear? Right, it's /oo/, do we remember how we spelled that /oo/ sound in the word TO? Yes with an O." /d/ is spelled with a D. /ā/ is spelled with the Vowel Team -AY.
grow	3	/g/ /r/ //ō/
show	2	/sh/ /ō/
own	2	/ō/ /n/
yellow	4	/y/ /ĕ/ /l/ /ō/
know	2	Say, "What sound do we hear first? Yes, /n/, how do we usually spell /n/? Perfect with an N, though in this word we are going to use -KN." /ō/ is spelled with -OW.
don't	4	/d/ is spelled with a D, /ō/ is spelled with an O, /n/ is spelled with a N, and /t/ is spelled with a T, Say, "What is this word called again? Yes, (don't) this is actually two words put together "do" and "not", and when we put them together we get "don't" and we need to add an apostrophe after the -N and before the -T."
right	3	/r/ /ī/ /t/
light	3	/l/ /ī/ /t/
eight	2	Say, "The first sound we hear is? Yes, /ā/, and how do we typically spell that? Correct with an -A, but in this word we will be using -EIGH." /t/ is spelled with a T.

Unit 4

This cheat sheet will help you know how words are mapped and what do to when teaching words with an irregular sound spelling.

Word	Number of Sounds	Sounds to Spell
all	2	/aw/ /l/
fall	3	/f/ /aw/ /l/
ball	3	/b/ /aw/ /l/
small	4	/s/ /m/ /aw/ /l/
full	3	/f/ /ŭ/ /l/
pull	3	/p/ ŭ/ /l/
also	4	/aw/ /l/ /s/ /ō/
always	5	/aw/ /l/ /w/ /ā/ /z/
walk	**3**	/w/ is spelled with a W. **Say, "What sound do we hear next? Yes /aw/, how have we been spelling that sound, yes with an A, but in this word it is going to be –AL."** /k/ is spelled with a K.
kind	4	/k/ /ī/ /n/ /d/
old	3	/ō/ /l/ /d/
cold	4	/k/ /ō/ l/ /d/
hold	4	/h/ /ō/ /l/ /d/
find	4	/f/ /ī/ /n/ /d/
far	2	/f/ /ar/
part	3	/p/ /ar/ /t/
start	4	/s/ /t/ /ar/ /t/

Word	Number of Sounds	Sounds to Spell
are	1	Say, "What sound do we hear? Yes, /ar/, how do we spell that sound usually? Perfect, with –AR, but this has a silent e attached so we will spell it -ARE."
carry	4	/k/ is spelled with a C. Say, "What is the next sound we hear? Yes, it's a tricky one /aŕ/, we are going to spell that sound with –ARR. And what's the last sound we hear? Yes, /ē/, how do we usually spell that? Perfect with an E, but when we hear the /ē/ sound at the end of a word, we typically use a Y."
warm	3	/w/ is spelled with a W. Say, "What's the next sound? Yes /or/, how do we spell that? Usually with a –OR, but in this word it is –AR." /m/ is spelled with an M
or	1	/or/
for	2	/f/ /or/
more	3	/m/ /ō/ /r/
before	5	/b/ /ē/ /f/ /ō/ /r/
work	3	/w/ is spelled with a W. Say, "What is the second sound we hear? Correct /er/, how is that typically spelled? Correct, with -ER, but in this word we will be using –OR." /k/ is spelled with a K
your	2	/y/ is spelled with a Y. Say, "What do we hear next? Yes, we hear /or/, how is that usually spelled? Correct, we typically use –OR, but we will use –OUR for this word."
four	2	/f/ is spelled with an F. Say, "The next sound we hear is… Yes, /or/. What do we usually use to spell /or/? Perfect we do us –OR but in this number word we use –OUR, this makes it different from the word "for" we already learned and connects to the number."
her	2	/h/ /er/
hers	3	/h/ /er/ /z/
after	4	/ă/ /f/ /t/ /er/
under	4	/ŭ/ /n/ /d/ /er/

Word	Number of Sounds	Sounds to Spell
better	4	/b/ /ĕ/ /t/ /er/
number	5	/n/ /ŭ/ /m/ /b/ /er/
over	3	/ō/ /v/ /er/
never	4	/n/ /ĕ/ /v/ /er/
very	4	/v/ is spelled with a V. **Say, "What is the next sound we hear; it might be a little hard to hear? Yes, it is /ă/ and how can we spell that sound? Yes with −A or −AY, but −AY is typically at the end of the word. In this word we use −E."** /r/ is spelled with an R. **Say, "It looks like −ER but does not say /er/ in this word. The last sound is? Perfect, /ē/, and we usually spell that with...−E, but like we talked about when we hear /ē/ at the end it is usually stolen by −Y."**
were	2	/w/ is spelled with a W. **Say, "What is that last sound? Yes, /er/, how do we spell that. Yes with −ER, but in this word we use −ERE and will heart that part."**
together	6	/t/ is spelled with a T. **Say, "What is the next sound? Yes, it is /oo/. We might not remember or have learned how to spell this sound, but in this word we will use −O. Let's heart it so we can help us remember."** /g/ is spelled with a G, /ĕ/ is spelled with an E, /<u>th</u>/ is spelled with −TH, and /er/ is spelled with −ER.
other	3	**Say, "What's the first sound we hear? Perfect, it is /ŭ/, and how do we usually spell that sound? Yes, with a −U, but in this word we will use −O."** /<u>th</u>/ is spelled with −TH, and /er/ is spelled with −ER.
every	4	/ĕ/ is spelled with an E and /v/ is spelled with a V. **Say, "What sound do we hear next? Correct, it is /r/, we usually spell that sound with... Yes, −R, but in this word we will use −ER. And, we hear what sound at the end? Yes, /ē/, and do we remember what steals that sound... Yes, −Y."**
first	4	/f/ /er/ /s/ /t/
hurt	3	/h/ /er/ /t/
girl	3	/g/ /er/ /l/

Word	Number of Sounds	Sounds to Spell
there	3	/<u>th</u>/ is spelled with –TH. **Say, "What is the next sound we hear? Yes, it is /ā/; its kind of hidden with the next sound. How do we usually spell that? Perfect with an –A or –AY at the end of words. For this word we will use –E. What is the last sound? Yes /r/, we usually spell that with? Yes –R, but with "there" we will use –RE."**
where	3	/wh/ is spelled with –WH. **Say, "What is the next sound we hear? Yes, it is /ā/, just like in the word "there." How do we usually spell that? Perfect, with an –A or –AY at the end of words. For this word we will use –E. What is the last sound? Yes /r/, we usually spell that with? Yes –R, we will use –RE."**
their	3	/<u>th</u>/ is spelled with –TH. **Say, "What is the next sound we hear? Yes, it is /ā/. How do we usually spell that? Perfect, with an –A or –AY at the end of words. For this word we will use –E. What is the last sound? Yes /r/, we usually spell that with? Yes –R, but with this word we are going to use –IR."**

Unit 5

This cheat sheet will help you know how words are mapped and what do to when teaching words with an irregular sound spelling.

Word	Number of Sounds	Sounds to Spell
funny	4	/f/ /ŭ/ /n/ /ē/
only	4	/ō/ /n/ /l/ /ē/
many	4	/m/ is spelled with an M. **Say, "What sound do we hear next? Correct, we hear /ĕ/ and we typically spell that with... Yes –E, but in this word we will use an –A and heart that part."** /n/ is spelled with an N. /ē/ is spelled with a Y.
any	3	**Say, "What is the first sound we hear? Correct, we hear /ĕ/ and we typically spell that with... Yes –E, but in this word we will use an –A and heart that part."** /n/ is spelled with an N. /ē/ is spelled with a Y.
pretty	5	/p/ is spelled with a P. /r/ is spelled with an R. **Say, "What do we hear next? Yes, ĭ/, which we usually spell with... Yes –I, but in this word we will use –E and heart it."** /t/ is spelled with -TT (rabbit rule). /ē/ is spelled with a Y.
my	2	/m/ /ī/
why	2	/wh/ /ī/
by	2	/b/ /ī/
fly	3	/f/ /l/ /ī/
try	3	/t/ /r/ /ī/
sky	3	/s/ /k/ /ī/
myself	6	/m/ /ī/ /s/ /ĕ/ /l/ /f/
buy	2	/b/ is spelled with a B. **Say, "What is the last sound we hear? Yes, /ī/ and when we hear that at the end of a word, how do we usually spell it? Perfect, with –Y, but in this word we will use –UY and heart it."**

Word	Number of Sounds	Sounds to Spell
too	2	/t/ and /oo/
soon	3	/s/ /oo/ /n/
new	2	/n/ is spelled with an N. **Say, "What sound do we hear next? Yes, /oo/, we usually spell that with –OO, but in this word we will use –EW."**
blue	3	/b/ is spelled with a B, /l/ is spelled with an L. **Say, "Can you tell me the last sound in the word? Correct /oo/, and this is usually spelled with? Yes –OO, but for this color word it is –UE."**
good	3	/g/ /oo/ /d/
look	3	/l/ /oo/ /k/
took	3	/t/ /oo/ /k/
saw	2	/s/ /aw/
draw	3	/d/ /r/ /aw/
because	5	/b/ is spelled with a B, /ē/ is spelled with an E, /k/ is spelled with a C. **Say, "The next sound we hear is… Yes, /ŭ/, and we typically spell that with? Yes, –U but in this word we are using –AU which is our heart part."** /z/ is spelled with an S.
how	2	/h/ /ow/
now	2	/n/ /ow/
down	3	/d/ /ow/ /n/
brown	4	/b/ /r/ /ow/ /n/
round	4	/r/ /ow/ /n/ /d/
about	4	/ŭ/ /b/ /ow/ /t/
out	2	/ow/ /t/
our	2	/ow/ /r/
found	4	/f/ /ow/ /n/ /d/

Wrapping Up

Ready, Set, Read On! Your Next Steps and Staying in Touch

We hope you found this book to be an easy, practical read with tools that you can use with your child or your students tomorrow. While we covered a lot, I do want to remind you that this is definitely not an all-inclusive book. Our hope is that this gives you a starting point when working with early or struggling readers.

If you are a teacher like us who was not explicitly taught how to teach kids to read effectively, remember that you do not know better until you do! The good news is that if we follow what the evidence says, 95% of kids *can* learn to read.

Also remember that while much of what is considered the Science of Reading is established, it is still science, and new research is always emerging. We try to attend as many webinars and conferences as we can. We also like to follow the researchers on social media or their websites so we can stay up to date.

We hope you will join Heidi on social media or stay tuned to our website as we continue to share everything we learn and unlearn. Remember, this is a journey! Even well-known researchers and scientists are learning new things all the time.

If you are looking for more support, resources, and training in the Science of Reading, check out LitFlix! We have created this space to give you the tools and the training you need to teach reading aligned to the research and evidence. We offer over 10,000 pages of resources (and growing) plus access to several training sessions each month. Learn more at www.scienceofreading101club.com.

Thank you for being open to change and sitting with some uncomfortable feelings as we learn and grow together. Change is not always easy. We often remind ourselves that teaching is not about us, it is about the kids.

We believe that together, we CAN change the literacy statistics!